THE
LITTLE
CROSS
IN MY
POCKET

THE
LITTLE
CROSS
IN MY
POCKET

E. WADE GREGORY, SR

XULON PRESS

Xulon Press
2301 Lucien Way #415
Maitland, FL 32751
407.339.4217
www.xulonpress.com

Unless otherwise indicated, Scripture quotations taken
from the Holy Bible, New International Version (NIV).
Copyright © 1973, 1978, 1984, 2011 by Biblica, Inc.™.
Used by permission. All rights reserved.

Scripture quotations taken from the Revised Standard
Version (RSV). Copyright © 1946, 1952, and 1971
the Division of Christian Education of the National
Council of the Churches of Christ in the United States
of America. Used by permission. All rights reserved.

Scripture quotations taken from the Living Bible (TLB).
Copyright © 1971 by Tyndale House Foundation. Used
by permission of Tyndale House Publishers Inc., Carol
Stream, Illinois 60188. All rights reserved.

Paperback ISBN-13: 978-1-6322-1538-3

Ebook ISBN-13: 978-1-6322-1539-0

CONTENTS

The Cross in My Pocket

I carry a cross in my pocket
A simple reminder to me
Of the fact that I am a Christian
No matter where I may be

This little cross is not magic
Nor is it a good luck charm
It is not meant to protect me
From every physical harm

It's not for identification
For all the world to see
It's simply an understanding
Between my Savior and me

When I put my hand in my pocket
To bring out a coin or a key
The cross is there to remind me
Of the price He paid for me

It reminds me too, to be thankful
For my blessings day by day
And strive to serve Him better
In all I do and say

It's also a daily reminder
Of the peace and comfort I share
With all who know my Master
And give themselves to His care

So I carry a cross in my pocket
Reminding no one but me
That Jesus Christ is Lord of my life
If only I'll let Him be

Verna Thomas

PREFACE

"For I am not ashamed of the Gospel of Christ"
Romans 1:16 NIV

There are so many family members, friends, teachers, professors, and even acquaintances for which my wife Onda and I will be forever grateful. We have eternal gratitude for what Christ Jesus has done for us and in our lives and the burden He has given us for others. As His servants, we were deployed in our own sphere of influence to share His love and be attentive to the needs of those around us. The Holy Spirit has been so patient, and is still teaching us how to share this wondrous love.

As a child and into adulthood, I was especially close to my grandfather, after whom I was named. I learned so much from this loving, gentle man and at the end of his life; even as he was breathing his last breaths he was teaching me. He had suffered a stroke and I stood by his hospital bed for hours just holding his hand and watching his heart monitor. Coming in and out of deep slumber, each time he would awake with a sense of panic, trying over and again to determine what had happened to him and where he was. I would respond every time, softly saying, "Grandpa, it's okay. I'm here. You are safe!" A silent smile would appear on his face and he would sink back into a deep sleep. I was repeatedly drawn to the heart monitor at the head of his bed as it would register his frenzy with rapid and erratic heart wave patterns. Yet, each time I spoke reassurance, the patterns would more and more return to normal. Often, as he would awake and look around the room, he would center his focus on the Crucifix hanging on the wall, saying, "He's so good."

While he had taught me so much about life, he was now teaching me the importance of "speaking to the heart". Every one of us has a heart monitor. I knew I would need to speak with gentleness to all people, in and with the love of the Lord whenever possible. Soon I would be slipping a little pocket cross into his casket, and these were the thoughts going through my mind; the heart monitor, talking to "hearts", and the little cross etched with "God loves you" and with that my own, "I love you too." I'll have an opportunity so say it again to him some day.

MY PRAYER

Loving Father,

I thank you for the life you have given us and the call you have placed on our lives . We are forever thankful for the opportunity you have given us to serve you and to share the love of Christ and the message He wishes to convey as we speak to the hearts of those you place in our path. I pray that if I have shared anything herein displeasing to you or that does not bring you honor, that it will be quickly forgotten.

This I ask in the name of the Lord Jesus, Amen.

Chapter One

"Called To The Family Business"

"May I never boast except in the cross of our Lord Jesus
Christ, through which the world has been crucified to
me and I to the world."
Galatians 6:14 NIV

I was a little taken aback some years ago when my five year
old grandson, Gabrien, called and said that he wanted
to marry the little girl next door to him. I asked, "When is
this supposed to happen?" He replied that he and the girl
had set a date for July 36th. "And where are the two of you
planning to live?" I asked. He must have given this some
thought because without hesitation he said, "We'll live at
my house part of the time and at her house part of the time."
"What do your parents have to say about all of this?" It was
becoming clear that his mother wasn't fully on board after

he confessed that she had told him his parents were not going to contribute any funds to a ring or a dress quite yet. But it was coming out in the conversation that he thought, maybe Grandpa would? "I'm putting July 36th on my calendar, you keep me posted!" I told my grandson. Today he is an Army officer and we are still waiting for July 36th to roll around.

Some decisions need time and should take time. But there are decisions each of us wish we might have made sooner. And still, there is our time table and there is God's time table. He does have plans for our lives, wonderful plans! But there are decisions in front of us every day that require a response. And ignoring a decision in front of us is often no better than backing out of an agreement. Often we enter an internal dialogue of "what ifs" and consider outcomes when it comes to obedience and faith. The fact that there is an argument going on in our mind, "Will I follow, will I do nothing?" shows how many conditions we need to have met before we will act in belief. This is a struggle, and yet it is very safe to say, for the follower of Christ, that we want his voice to win out over every competitor, that He would be first, and that we who have the mind of Christ would actually think and say, "Here am I".

As a child, I had attended a small Methodist church and had committed my life to Christ during a youth rally. About the same time my wife, Onda, who had been brought up in the EUB church, had also given her heart to Christ. We were high-school sweethearts who went on to be married and have been blessed with over fifty years of marriage and two children, Tami and Everett. At first, we were not as involved in church life but eventually we decided to go back to that same little Methodist church where I met Christ. Little did we know that our involvement would lead us both to full time ministry in the pastorate. There were a few years of just trying to be the best lay-people we could be but it wasn't until a lay witness meeting where the two of us found ourselves on our knees with renewed determination to live for Christ, praying specifically, that we would become "good and faithful" servants of the Lord. And there, at that altar, we each picked up a little cross with the engraved words, "God Loves You."

It has taken a lifetime to begin to grasp the depth of His love and how we were to love others as Christ loves us. We knew that our Lord and Savior desired us to share that love with everyone. Onda and I cherished the little cross we each carried. Hers in her purse, mine in my pocket.

We both felt that we would carry that little cross for the rest of our lives. We can't recall to whom we gave our cross, but soon we would in like manner encounter others with brokenness and need and would present them with a cross saying, "God loves you and so do I." Then and now, some Christians might find such a practice trite, but when a Christian, knowing the love of God towards themselves, and for all mankind, "speaks to the heart", into the heart of a person with the love of Jesus, things happen! Good things.

We had a friend who used to say, "God loves you and I'm trying." It's unsettling, to learn that loving people is not optional, because some people are hard to love. And yet, the Lord Jesus, pouring out his love to His disciples at the Last Supper, commanded that we were to love others as He loved them. This is just hours before He would be nailed to the Cross to suffer for our sins. I confess, loving people as Christ loves us, is difficult and it is no small undertaking. I was carrying my little pocket cross but I also carried a gun and a badge. A good many of the people I encountered were not particularly "lovable" but there was never any doubt that Jesus loved them. It was not until I attempted to look at them through the eyes of Christ that I too could love the so-called "unlovable".

Everyone needs to be loved and when they receive and accept the fact that God truly loves them, it makes all the difference in the world. To convey this message, I discovered that the little cross in my pocket provided an opening that worked hundreds of times with little resistance. Even when being a police officer demanded coming face to face with what evil men do, I didn't have any hatred for the perpetrators. Sticks and stones actually do break bones and so do lawn chairs being thrown at you and my colleagues, but I didn't hate them, only their actions. If Christ can forgive those who nailed him to a cross so must I when I might be experiencing persecution or abuse.

Giving away a pocket cross, for Onda and I, was appropriate just part of the time. We weren't blanketing an area with tracts and crosses. It may have seemed like a good idea to pass out crosses like advertisements but we were following the lead of the Holy Spirit. The Scripture calls it discernment. We did not grab anyone by the nap of their neck, threatening them with hellfire. Our leading, the job description, called for us to be His servants, witnesses and not consultants. And we were being deployed in our own back-yard, or wherever He would lead us.

The scene at the Last Supper according to the Gospel of John shows Jesus washing the feet of his disciples. The Lord showed them that this was their role, as being His, servant. The washing of the feet was an act of consecration. Paul said, "Blessed are the feet of those who come proclaiming Good News."(Rom 10:15NIV) God had sent out a rescue party of One, His Son, Jesus Christ to save the world. Those called by the Lord are called into the "Family Business" of sharing God's word and His love. The Gospel is for all to experience and it is especially for those who have never heard, or sadly, for many who have heard but never felt the love of God.

As Christians, we are called into His service and into roles as assigned by the Lord. (Eph. 4:11-12) His disciples are constantly being deployed as will be seen in many of the stories that will be shared. Onda and I did not have to go looking for someone to share with or to present them with the little cross that says, "God loves you." They often showed up on the doorstep or "out of the clear blue sky." They often had a specific need, were struggling, even sometimes in pain, and there they were. As servants of the King, we sought guidance from the Holy Spirit. We also were aware that we might only be able to offer "spiritual first aid" and with discernment perhaps refer them to others whose skills were needed. There was one occasion that a man showed up at the front door with a knife in his back.

Apparently his significant other had gotten really mad at him. My training as an EMT came in handy many times.

While I consider the role of a disciple or a servant as a calling, this ministry is not always easy when there are so many scoffers. Walking into a co-worker's office one day, he suddenly turned to me and said, "Well (expletive)!" I quickly replied, "No, just one of His ambassadors." Paul wrote to Corinth in 2 Cor. 5:19-20 NIV that, "God was reconciling the world to Himself in Christ, not counting people's sins against them. And He has committed $_{to\ us}$ the message of reconciliation." We are therefore Christ's ambassadors, Embassy representatives. In this role I have to admit, I have had to bite my tongue many times. In the stories shared herein, the focus is on Christ, and not me. After many years I am reminded that years of being a police officer, numerous criminal investigations, a juvenile parole agent, a family and youth counselor, a registered social worker, a chaplain, eight years an EMT, and thirty years as an United Methodist Pastor, I am still a work in progress, "under construction". So, if there is any encouragement to gain, may Christ be glorified because, "Not I, but Christ in me... who loved me, and gave Himself for me."

TRUST AND OBEY

When we walk with the Lord In the light of His Word,
What a glory He sheds on our way! While we do His
good will,
He abides with us still, And with all who trust and obey.
Trust and o–bey, For there's no other way
To be happy in Jesus, but to trust and o – bey.

James H. Sammis

Chapter Two

ONLY GOD CAN
HEAL A BROKEN HEART

"I want you to call to me in your day of trouble so that
I can rescue you and you will give me glory!"
Psalm 50:7 (TLB)

Everyone ought to have a coffee shop where they can enjoy a good cup of coffee, a meal, and especially the fellowship of family, friends, and neighbors. My wife and I have enjoyed this part of our lives and it has become a part of our ministry that we have shared together and on occasion separately. It was always a joy, this time together and with those in our community. When serendipitous, providential encounters happened, they were often spontaneous, unplanned. We didn't assume that every time we entered our "spot" that something supernatural was about to take place.

But often when we make contact with other people we would discover our "mission" for the day.

On one particular visit we were confronted with a person we had seen before. on various occasions. This was a familiar scenario, as the woman approached us Onda leaned over and said "Something is seriously wrong here I sense a great deal of pain in her this morning. Let's give her one of our little crosses and tell her we appreciate her and love her." Trusting my wife's insight, as I reached out and put the little pocket cross in her hand and said, "It says that God loves you!" Onda quickly added, "You look a little blue, and just know, we love you too." With this, she started weeping. After a few moments passed, she lifted her face and said, "I'm glad someone does! My husband told me this morning that he doesn't love me anymore and wants a divorce." As we had done so many times before on previous occasions, we could only hold her hands and tell her "God truly does love you and will never leave you or forsake you." We heard later that there were others there for her as well. It took months before her usual cheerfulness was back on display.

There is nothing more devastating than a sense of hope-lessness. Fear rushes in. Insecurity is crippling and the heart is breaking. As for many of these, broken marriages and the cruel feeling of betrayal play on the mind and heart. To give love and have that love rejected or interrupted abruptly and dramatically, can break and traumatize the heart. A heart attack works like this and it leaves damage. Prayerfully, per-sonal disasters cannot be repaired until we realize that only God can heal a broken heart. We Christians cannot rescue people from such brokenness and pain but we can point them to the One who can and will. The servant/witness, they are ready to be available to the leading of the Holy Spirit to reach out in love to those in need.

It is important to stress that one of the gifts of the Spirit is discernment as it relates to ministering to others. Knowing how to respond to a need, how God wants us to meet that need, in and through His love, this is discernment. There have been times when both the gift of discernment and even the word of knowledge have come into play when Onda and I ministered to others. We cannot claim any special ability of our own, it is the work of the Holy Spirit

There are times when the Spirit of God inserts Himself into our lives, makes us very aware of what He wants of us, so that we will intersect with the life of another – another whom He loves and seeks. We hide and Jesus seeks, but He seeks through us. It's a matter of having our path, our routine, redirected, open to interruption, so that we go where He wants us to go. He expects us to be ready to do his bidding. There are times perhaps when we might not want to go to what we may perceive as nothing less than a war zone. Life is messy. We would rather relax ourselves right into eternity. But our ministry is reconciliation not relaxation. Jonah did not want to go where God was sending him. He was only happy so long as his scrawny tree let him sit in the shade. Imagine a cavalry soldier in Custer's 7th Calvary saying, "Hey General, I don't want to go." The servant goes, as our Lord Jesus went, because it's His mission and now because it's our mission. This is the Family Business. We want to be obedient disciples of Christ.

I remember those times that I had to reverse where I was headed or what I was doing in the moment, because, I just had to. The discernment didn't always kick in immediately, but eventually after I arrived at where I was supposed to be, it did. Sometimes I had to excuse myself from a meal, a meeting, or something that I was doing and didn't know until later why I had to go where I was being directed. I often found myself at a home, a hospital, a nursing home, or back at church to find a specific need to be there, waiting for me. After visiting someone at the hospital, I would be compelled, almost controlled, to return immediately to find that a "Code Blue" (cardiac arrest) was happening to one of my flock. This wasn't a cell phone alert dinging or vibrating in my pocket. The "vibrations" were from somewhere else. Or I would arrive at what I thought to be a sort of routine visit to a nursing home while at the exact same time a nurse had just found one of the members of our church to have stopped breathing or to have been in the middle of a panic attack. It was not uncommon to be asked by a patient, a nurse, or a family member, "Why are you here already?" or "How did you know?"

On one occasion, out of seemingly nowhere, Onda jumped up from our living room chair and said, "I have to go!" When I asked, "Where are you going?" she replied, "I don't know for sure!" It was not until she got into the car that she was directed to our friend Ruth's home. When she got there, she could see smoke and walking on in; she immediately searched for the source of the smoke. Ruth was blind and did not realize that a neighbor who had brought her some food had placed it in her oven with hot pads. When she turned on the oven to heat the meal up, the pads had caught fire. Astonished, Ruth asked Onda how she knew to come to her home at that particular time. Ruth was in a dire situation, in need of rescuing and Onda was available and thus, deployed. Onda told her that she didn't know why she came until she got to the front door.

Maybe we are not supposed to fully understand why Gods asks us to do certain biddings. Perhaps someone would say to themselves that the fire was in an oven so she would have been alright. That's more than a little cold and callous. But what if our blind Ruth tried fixing the situation herself? What if Ruth's house filled with enough smoke that she panicked and had a heart attack? Or what if the fire reached the vent on the top of the oven where a kitchen towel was laying? We're not to ask why, or to ask about potentialities, about if and why and how and what then? We are just to do what He says. There is real joy knowing that God will use us and in all cases, He gets all the credit and glory. We are not to call attention to what we do for the Lord.

We share that which God does for us and for others. God does not take us for granted and we do not take Him for granted. We are to be like the employee that knows their job description and completes all the assigned tasks. The employee does not ask for special favor for doing what is expected of them but should take satisfaction and joy for being a loyal and faithful worker. It's sort of interesting that there are those who need praise and positive strokes just to do what is expected of them. We do, however, want to praise and show appreciation to those who are really doing a good job.

The athletes who trains every day, travels constantly, compete strategically are the people that our culture often praises most. And what are they really doing? Their job! The goal of an athlete in the Olympics is to "bring home the Gold". That "bringing home" is the goal of the Christian. We bring home glory to God and we glory in God because He is our home.

In all of life, Christians are asked to make themself available to the Lord Jesus. There is a risk in a prayer for God to use us if we don't consider the fact that God might say "Okay, I will!" Maybe this is what Paul meant when he told the Church in his letter, "Be ready...being urgent in season and out of season. Be ready to tell them!"(2Tim4:2) What do we tell them? "God loves you!" And hopefully, we can say, "We do too", because they will know the difference. When someone either says aloud, "I love you too", or if they communicate it authentically in their voice, in their eyes, in their expressions, the "God loves you" takes on flesh, God's love is "fleshed" out.

As with those who hearts are breaking, God does want to rescue us when we call out to Him. He doesn't necessarily take us out of our difficulty but promises He will go through it with us. He wants to heal the brokenhearted and embrace us with His wholeness. He even will send a servant who He will equip to help out along the way, and that servant may be you!

A Prayer

Loving Father,

There are so many times you have rescued us even from ourselves. You have revealed yourself through the Holy Spirit. Your promises are true, and we hold on to them with all our love. You have given us so many gifts that too often we did not even recognize them at the time. Forgive us, Lord, of our failings and accept our eternal gratitude for all that You do. Thank You for healing the broken-hearted. In Christ we pray. Amen

Chapter Three

"CHRIST IS THE ANSWER...
BUT WHAT IS THE QUESTION?"

"Jesus asked his disciples, 'Who do people say the Son
of Man is?' They replied, "Some say John the Baptist,
Elijah...or one of the Prophets."
Then Jesus asked, "Who do you say that I am"
Matt. 16:14 – 16 NIV

Before seminary and the pastorate, there were fourteen
years of Law Enforcement and Juvenile Corrections.
These were fulfilling years professionally, but also difficult
years. Working with troubled youth on parole from insti-
tutions in the State of Illinois was rewarding but at times,
very trying. I was a former police officer, now a juvenile
parole agent, a certified family and youth counselor, and a
registered social worker. It was not always easy to balance
the role of counselor and occasional disciplinarian, with

authority to send a youngster back to a juvenile facility, while at the same time committed to being a compassionate Christian. At the time, there were more experts in juvenile delinquency than there were juvenile delinquents. There were many philosophies which dealt with the problems of young people who committed crimes or violated court ordered supervision. The truth was these were youth who committed violent or even heinous crimes, as well as rebellious minors who refused to go to school as part of their court ordered probation. They had all failed to conform to society's expectations and would be subject to many different rehabilitation programs. Too often the programs were changed or just faded away without any real or follow up evaluation as to their merits or failures. In each case however, there was a sincere attempt to affect change in these youngster's behavior.

There was never any doubt that those responsible for providing housing and treatment for these who were socially and sometimes mentally handicapped were always working hard to provide answers to one of society's worse problems. It might be difficult to understand that some of our most hardened criminals could be younger than fifteen years old. But some were.

In parole work, I found that some of the best resources available for community-based programs were churches and Christian people in addition to local community agencies. It was Christian people who were often willing to open their homes to provide housing and care for youth who had no acceptable home to return to following institutionalization.

Some of the communities would even refuse to take them back.

The most common denominator among these kids was that they did not have a stable home environment. Also, they were not always particularly lovable but needed love in the worse way. This is what is usually called, "tough love." While it was not advisable, Onda and I often had some of these young people in our home and on occasion, would take them to special events which might appeal to young people.

It was one such occasion that three of four youth I had placed in a group home that I had established wanted to go to see Billy Graham's movie production of "Time to Run." At the last minute, the fourth teen declared he wanted to go as well. While nothing was said throughout the movie, at the end of the showing, there was an invitation given if anyone desired to commit their lives to Christ. To our complete surprise, three of our young parolees jumped out of their seats and literally ran to the front of the theater and asked the Lord to come into their lives.

Before leaving for the movie, Onda had placed three cross necklaces made with nails, in her purse. She said later that she had no specific expectations but only picked up three even though we had four teens going with us to the movie. The three adolescents were visibly excited as Onda placed the crosses around their necks. They were talking about how their lives flashed before them and how they really wanted to turn over a new leaf in their lives. They had heard about Jesus before, but had little understanding that might have come earlier from church attendance. Now they wanted to make this commitment. The fourth teen, Steve, who decided to attend at the last moment, did not go forward but was extremely upset, visibly angered about not receiving a cross to wear. He wanted a cross but indicated that the movie and invitation did not speak to him.

Later at the group home, we had a group discussion with the foster mother about how the three new Christians could contribute to the home. They would find and attend a church that the three of them could go together. Steve, still dejected over not getting a cross, wanted to know why he could not have one. I told him that the cross represented something very special to Vern, Bill, and Tommy. It was explained that they had a new understanding about what they wanted in their lives and that for them, "JESUS WAS THE ANSWER." The Cross is often reduced to nothing but a fashionable piece of jewelry but the crosses the boys were given were not something merely to wear but to bear. The Cross of Christ is the love of God, and our cross, is the love of God for God.

"Steve," I said, "Jesus is the answer." Steve stood up and leaned over the kitchen table and said, "Jesus is the answer Mr. Gregory, but what is the question?"

Here was a young man who needed an answer perhaps more so than the others, for he truly needed to experience the love of the Lord. He had come from a terrible home situation and his acting out was a result of tremendous pain from feeling totally rejected by his parents, his school, and his community. This was no excuse for his actions in his young life, but his problems were understandable.

For the next few weeks, I found myself loving Steve all the more for his inner pain was so severe and his occasional acting out was being brought to my attention. I loved this kid but at the same I would like to wring his neck–in love of course.

It was during one of our private conversations that Steve brought up our prior discussion about, "Jesus is the answer." Steve said, "I still don't get it!" I asked Steve if he knew what the first question that God asked man in the Bible. Steve said, "NO!" I went on to tell him that the Bible says that the first recorded question God asked was of Adam. "Adam! Where are you?"(Gen.3:9NIV) "Steve," I said, "God knew where the man he created and loved was. He knew that Adam had disobeyed him by doing something that God had strictly forbidden him to do. Adam thought he knew better and he wanted to hide from God because he had sinned against God."

"Steve, I believe God is still asking that same question of us all...He's asking like; "Steve, where are you? Steve you have not only been hiding from God, you've been hiding from yourself. You've needed to know someone loved you, with no conditions, with no strings, completely, and that person is Jesus Christ. Your friends here at the home have discovered this and have chosen Him as their Lord and are trying to involve him in their lives and future."

"Now for the answer to the first question the Bible (Gen.3:9,4:9)tells us that what man asked God was, 'Am

I my brother's keeper?' This was Cain, the son of Adam and Eve, who had killed his brother Abel out of hatred and jealousy. Now God knew that Cain had committed this heinous crime so when He asked Cain where was Abel, he answered God, 'Am I my brother's keeper?' Cain thought he could hide the murder and was being proud and sarcastic. As for God's answer to Cain's question about being his brother's keeper, it is to be found throughout the Old and New Testaments. From Genesis to Revelation, the last book of the Bible, God is telling us that we are our brother's keeper. He tells us that we are to care for others. He sent his only Son, Jesus Christ, to show us that He loved us so much that He gave up His life on the Cross so that we could live in a restored, eternal relationship with him."

"Steve, this is why you were not given a cross, for you have spent seventeen years of living just for yourself. You are a sensitive young man who has made a lot of sad mistakes and you need to know that you are loved, so much. Steve, Jesus is your answer!" He said very little after this but indicated that he was going to to think about what I said. He also said that he would talk to the others in the home in hope that this would help in his understanding. I told him that it was still inappropriate to give him a nail cross to wear around his neck but that I had a little cross that says, "God Loves You!" I hoped that he would carry it as he pondered on this which we had discussed.

I wish that I could share that Steve did become a committed Christian. Bill, Vern, and Tom went on to be discharged from parole supervision as did Steve. The three boys melted back into society and have not been heard from. Steve sort of floundered even though he married a Christian girl who deeply loved him. Onda and I shed many tears when we learned that Steve had succumbed to a deep and deadly depression and had committed suicide.

Jesus is truly the answer. Steve could or would not embrace that he was loved and failed to recognize this truth in his young life. Jesus is the answer. And the question God is still asking all of us, "Where are you?" Are we rejecting His love and living for ourselves? Or, are we trying to live for Him and serving others as Christ has commanded us? The question, "Where are you?" is an awkward question to say the very least. It's a, "you've been caught" sort of feeling. And the temptation to hear that voice and to think it a mean voice, for some is overwhelming. But the voice calling to us, whether to embrace Christ initially or to obey Christ now, is the voice of Love because "God is Love." (1John 4:16) When we reject the Love of God, we not only reject God, we ultimately reject ourselves. Oh, how we should pray that all will experience Christ's love and share His love. This all will come to fruition and find healing and wholeness.

A PRAYER

Our Father, we truly ache for those who have fallen into deep despair and hopelessness. Sin is such a horrible sickness and the burden we feel for those around us is nothing like the heartache you experience when those, whom You love, reject You. We are so thankful that these things are in your loving hands and our hearts are full of joy that You have showed us the answer is in Christ Jesus. Amen

Chapter Four

"LORD! I NEED SOME HELP IN HERE!"

"You call on the name of your god, and I will call on the name of the Lord. The god who answers by fire-He is God."
1 Kings 1:24 NIV

During the years I was a state juvenile parole agent, I spent most of my time in the field supervising and counseling youth declared delinquent by the court. I had also spent time visiting various detention facilities and jails throughout the State of Illinois. I had even visited similar facilities and juvenile programs in other states.

For a short period of time, I had an office located in one of our community based detention facilities. It was on one occasion while I was stationed at this unit that I was asked to provide supervision for a few detainees so that the entire institutional staff could have a meeting in another part of the building. In other words, I was asked to babysit so the staff could meet without the usual interruptions associated with the youth on the unit.

And on this particular day I did not want to be "unhinged" when a boy ran into my office and said, "You better come quick Mr. Gregory, Joe is trying to kill himself." As I followed him to Joe's room, I asked, "What is up with Joe?" The reply was that Joe had messed up pretty badly on the unit and was to be sent back to another institution which to him meant "hard time."

When I walked into Joe's room, I was surprised to see that he was sitting, cutting himself with what appeared to be a piece of glass from a broken light bulb. "Joe, give me the glass!" As I spoke to him, Joe looked up and raised his hand with the glass and shook it at me saying, "Stay away! I'm going to kill myself!" There was blood on the bed and on his wrist. The question I immediately asked myself was, "Is he going to cut me too if I get too close?" The next thought was, "Lord! I need help in here!" Sometimes the most effective prayer is the one word, "Help!" This would not have been the first time I would have to disarm an assailant with a weapon but hopefully there would be a way to do so without hurting Joe or spilling some of my own blood in the process.

"What do I say to Joe, Lord?" Then to my complete surprise, the words came out of my mouth, "Joe, you must be as dumb as those old prophets of Baal!" I thought to myself, "What in the world am I talking about?" "Joe, you know who those old prophets of Baal were, don't you?" Joe looked a little stunned as he shook his head no.

"Well Joe, way back in the Bible (1Kings18), there was a man of God named Elijah and a nasty old queen called Jezebel. Well, this woman and her old man, King Ahab had been killing off God's prophets, the good guys and Elijah told Jezebel and her crew they should have a showdown on a nearby mountain top to prove to all who was the one true God. The prophets of Baal were there, part of Jezebel's gang, and they were to prepare a burnt sacrifice on wood piles. One pile was for the Baal gods and the other pile was for the Lord God. Then Elijah said, "Let's find out who really is the true God. You guys call on your god to fire up your pile of wood." I still had Joe's attention and again I thought to myself, "I can't wait to hear myself how this all turns out."

"Well Joe," I said, "Those prophets of Baal, around 450 of them, jumped up and down, whooping and hollering, calling to their god Baal to send down fire. They even cut themselves to get Baal's attention. They cut themselves in desperation, but nothing happened. Elijah said, 'It's my turn!' He then had some dudes to pour water all over his wood pile a bunch of times and then he stopped and prayed to the Lord God. He wanted to prove how much better God was by making the wood all wet and impossible to light. And guess what? The fire came down and set the wood ablaze. Now everyone knew that the God of Elijah was the one true God. Then the people who had witnessed what had happened did a number on all the false prophets of Baal."

I really felt like I was on a roll when I told this young hopeless kid, "Joe, you have been trying to get a false god's attention by cutting yourself. You are seeking attention for help from a false god. The Lord that I know is the Lord in the Bible, the one and only true God. You need to know that He loves you and that He doesn't want you to harm yourself. It won't be easy, but the Lord can and will help you through your problems. I don't want you to just give me that glass, but I would like to trade you the glass for a little cross that I have here that says, "God loves You!" There was no hesitation. Joe handed me the glass and accepted the cross. He continued to look at it as I washed his wound and found a bandage to wrap his wrist.

The Lord never fails to amaze me. I just love it when He gives me and others the right words to say in rough times. Jesus said that He would. All I had was the good sense to say, "Lord! I need some help in here!" It is doubtful that the world will ever understand the working of the Holy Spirit or the power of love until such a time these things are revealed on that last assigned day.

Looking back in my life, I have accepted the fact that the Christian experience is one of common sense and practical application. All we have to do is call on Him. The world is full of "Joes" worshiping at the altar of false gods and in spiritual bondage.

The "Little Cross in My Pocket" is there to remind me that I too have been rescued from bondage by His love. He can "set the captive free" if we call out, "Lord!" I need some help in here!"

The Next Prayer!

"THANK YOU JESUS!"
I BELIEVE

I BELIEVE IN GOD, WHO IS FOR ME SPIRIT,
LOVE, AND THE PRINCIPAL OF ALL THINGS.
I BELIEVE THAT GOD IS IN ME, AS I AM IN HIM.
I BELIEVE THAT THE TRUE WELFARE OF MAN
CONSISTS IN FULLING THE WILL OF GOD.
I BELIEVE THAT FROM THE FULFILLMENT
OF THE WILL OF GOD THERE CAN FOLLOW
NOTHING BUT THAT WHICH IS GOOD FOR
ME FOR AND ALL MEN. I BELIEVE THAT THE
WILL OF GOD IS THAT EVERY MAN SHOULD
LOVE HIS FELLOW MEN, AND SHOULD ACT
TOWARD OTHERS AS HE DESIRES THAT THEY
SHOULD ACT TOWARD HIM. I BELIEVE THAT
THE REASON OF LIFE IS FOR EACH OF US
SIMPLY GROW IN LOVE.
I BELIEVE THAT THIS GROWTH IN LOVE
WILL CONTRIBUTE MORE THAN ANY OTHER
FORCE TO ESTABLISH THE KINGDOM OF GOD
ON EARTH.

Leo Tolstoy

Chapter Five

"THE GOOD, THE BAD, AND THE OPPORTUNITY"

"For the eyes of the Lord are on the righteous...but the face of the Lord is against those who do evil...always be prepared to give an answer to everyone who asks you to give the reason for the hope that you have."
1 Peter 3:12, 15b NIV

For over fourteen years, I had seen the evil man could do against their fellow man. Before I traded a gun and badge for a cross and the Bible, there were those encounters with those who had committed heinous crimes, including sexual assault, arson, murder, and vicious beatings.

One such case involved a young man named Roger, who I worked with over a period of a few years. To converse with him, one would find him friendly and he did not come off as especially aggressive, let alone a violent person.

Roger liked to steal cars for joy rides and from a conservative estimate, probably stole ninety to one hundred cars in a period of four years.

By the time he was seventeen, he began committing strong armed and armed robberies. He always acted alone and his crimes became more and more violent by nature. He held up a service station and shot the attendant who barely survived.

Following this incident, he was spotted in a stolen car and an extended police car chase followed. He finally bailed out of the car and eluded police officers. I was in a state police plane with a police captain overhead a farm field when police officers on the ground found him in a drainage ditch. He was convicted of this crime and sentenced to prison, this time as an adult.

It was only about two and one-half years later that Roger was released on parole. In a matter of just a few days, Roger was arrested for murder. This time, he had stabbed a man in the throat with a knife and had disposed of the man's body out along the side of a road.

Needless to say, I was not particularly interested in talking to Roger again but because of Roger's past willingness to be open with me, I was asked to interview him regarding any other criminal activities he might have committed before being arrested for the most recent murder.

This time, I would interview Roger in his jail cell and limit the conversation to anything but his arrest and pending court appearance. When Roger saw me he laughed and said he was really glad to see me. I don't know if Roger could tell how uncomfortable I was being with him. He didn't seem to mind being with me. But he wanted to brag a little about some of the things he had done. His tone was similar to the one he had displayed following the shooting of the gas station attendant. On that occasion, Roger had admitted to me that he had robbed, beaten, and killed an old man on the street whose murder went undetected. He thought it was funny that it was not discovered during the funeral process that the man had been kicked to death. We had to exhume the body only to discover that Roger was telling the truth. Because of the delay and error, Roger was only charged with aggravated battery.

Now at his jail cell, I managed to not show my anger at his attitude by holding onto the cross that I held in my pocket. He thought it was funny that he had done so much "stuff" and had not gotten caught. Somehow, I found myself asking Roger if he knew that somewhere inside him there had to be some good. "After all, Roger, God still loves you and some day you will have to stand before the Judge of creation for the evil things you have done."

Roger continued to smile and insist that there was probably no good in him and that he was ready to go back to prison. The expression on his face could only be described as dark and convincingly evil. He finally said, "It's OK, Mr. Gregory!" I replied that he was not OK and surely he did not want his family to suffer the humiliation of seeing him being sent back to prison. Somehow, he couldn't be all that bad.

To my surprise, Roger then began to disclose and brag that he had killed some other fellow inmates in prison, and that the other prisoners would never mess with him. Roger wanted to show me how bad he was and to leave no doubt in me that he was in fact, hopeless, laughing as he spilled details. I ended the conversation by telling Roger that I wished he could have understood that God had a far different plan for his life. Smiling, he told me, "Don't worry about it."

Roger was still laughing as I turned to go but then there was another voice that called out to me. There was another prisoner in the adjoining cell and apparently, he had been listening to Roger and my conversation. "Hey, Mr. Gregory, I know what you have been telling Roger and I am beginning to understand some things about God and I'm going to tell him all "about it."

I had been clinching my little pocket cross all this time and when I saw the man in the next cell, I recognized him. I told him, "God loves you too. When you get released from here this little cross will be in your property sack. "I was headed to the jailer's desk to drop off the cross when I heard the man say, "Roger, you stupid ——!" Don't you know you are going to hell! You better listen up Dude!"

I didn't hear any more of the conversation but thought that God does have his ways to convey His message. This time a fellow prisoner was telling another prisoner that we do have to answer to God for all the things that we do and have done. There are hopefully a lot of good things in man, but even when there are a lot of bad things in us, there is still an opportunity. God will have his way with us eventually. One thing is for sure, that evil is ugly and a destroyer of souls.

It was no surprise that when I called my friend, Don, warden of Joliet State prison that he later confirmed that there had been some unsolved murders at the prison and from the details I had given him, Roger might well be responsible for all if not some of these murders.

One of the most disturbing passages in the Bible is when Jesus says, "When lawlessness spreads, man's love for one another will be waxed cold."(Matt.24:12KJV) The ability to maintain a loving nature is being constantly confronted by the evil forces in our world. We are witnessing every day such horrible things that mankind is committing. There is family against family, neighbor against neighbor, nation against nation, and religion against religion. Our ability to maintain our love comes only through the power of the Holy Spirit and the love we have for Christ with the desire to be obedient to Him. Christians need to pray that the flame of God's love will ignite in more and more hearts and that love will remain the anchor of our faith. There will be countless confrontations and there will be countless opportunities.

A PRAYER

Loving Father,

There are many times in our lives that it seems we are being buffeted by waves of fear and anger when exposed to the evil things people do to us and to good people around us. Deliver us from such evil that would penetrate our hearts and possibly cripple us from doing your will. Remind us that most, if not all battles belong to you and that Victory is ours through our Lord and Savior Jesus Christ. Amen

Chapter Six

"WITH GOD THERE ARE NO COINCIDENCES"

"Let the little children come to me and do not hinder them, for the kingdom of heaven belongs to such as these."
Matthew 19:14 NIV

As I was leaving a class at the seminary I was attending in Evanston, near Chicago, I was handed a note that said, "Call Ivan Eastman as soon as possible. This is an emergency!" Surprised and confused, I reread the note; the telephone number given seemed odd given it wasn't a familiar prefix. I immediately tried calling this number but kept getting a recorded message that the number that I was calling was not in service. I was using the area code of my community and concluded that the office secretary had written down an incorrect phone number. I called information and got Ivan's home phone number, but I got no answer. I called some other church members, but no one was aware of any emergency. There was no information of where Ivan and his wife Clara were, or if there were any problems.

As soon as I returned to our apartment, my wife and I tried again to call back home but to no avail. We joined our friends, fellow pastor and classmate, Jerry Ulin and wife, Judy and headed for the Brookfield Zoo in downtown Chicago. They joined us in prayer as we asked the Lord to be with the Eastman's in whatever emergency they had. We would again try calling them from the zoo.

One could imagine our surprise when we walked into the entrance of the zoo and here stood Ivan Eastman and his son-in-law Pete. They were just as surprised as we were when we explained that we had been trying to call them back home and had not reached anyone or had any information from church members where they were. Ivan went on to explain that he and Clara called from here in Chicago. They had rushed to a nearby hospital because their eight-year-old granddaughter Latreasa had been struck by a car and was in a coma. Ivan and Pete had just walked over to the zoo for a short break while Clara, and Mary, Latreasa's mother, remained with the unconscious girl in an intensive care room. With dozens of people milling around the entrance of the zoo, we all joined hands and prayed for Latreasa.

Jerry and I walked to the hospital with Ivan and Pete and joined the other family members at the little girl's bedside. There lay this child, white as a ghost and with labored breathing. We could only stay a few moments, but we prayed for Latreasa, holding onto her little limp hands.

I whispered a few words of comfort to Mary and I placed one of my little crosses in her hand. I told her, "God loves Latreasa, and you." I asked her to please give it to her when she wakes up. Even though she was in a life-threatening situation, I knew this child was in Jesus' hands as Jerry and I rejoined our wives at the zoo.

Between classes the following morning, I was able to contact Ivan at the Chicago phone number. When I asked how Latreasa was doing, Ivan was sobbing a little when he said, "She's awake and says she's hungry!" She wanted to know why she could not play with the other children on the children's ward. Ivan agreed with me that if God could bring us together in downtown Chicago, a metropolis of over four million people, he could heal one little girl. We also agreed that this was not a coincidence but a God incident.

Latreasa's recovery was truly miraculous but there was more to this story that involved her and her whole family. A few weeks later, Ivan, Clara, Latreasa, her parents, brothers, and sisters walked into the church on a Sunday morning. Latreasa immediately yelled out, "Wade!" and ran and jumped into my arms. This would become a usual occurrence every Sunday for the family had decided to move near to our rural Illinois Niantic community so that they could live in a safer environment and especially so that they could be near family members and the church. They made the transition and were welcomed with open arms. Every

Sunday, I had to brace myself when Latreasa came through the door.

A few months later, the opportunity was given to those who had committed their lives to Christ to be baptized by immersion. United Methodists acknowledge sprinkling, pouring, and baptism by immersion with the understanding that the Holy Spirit is the Baptizer. The church is entrusted with the blessing of administering the sacrament and giving people the choice of the method. Among those asking to receive the holy sacrament were Mary, Pete and of course, Latreasa. She loved Sunday school and her many church friends. She made it clear that she loved Jesus and wanted to make Him Lord of her young life.

There were about thirty people who came to a sister United Methodist Church, which had a baptistery. Another pastor friend had some from his church wishing baptism by immersion and we joined together in what was a time of much joy and celebration. It was humbling for so many persons shared of their faith and gathered around the baptistery in mutual love and support.

Latreasa had found a seat on the edge and sat there motionless and very attentive. When it came time for Pete, Mary, and Latreasa, I asked Pete to assist, for he was the spiritual head of his family and was expected to take a leadership role. Latreasa insisted that she wanted to be baptized but also made it clear that she was afraid of putting her head under the water. She finally agreed when I told her that we would go under the water together with me holding her tightly. We both went under, "In the name of the Father, the Son, and the Holy Spirit." When we came up, my brave little soul was all smiles.

In the weeks that followed Latreasa's mother and grandmother were both sharing that Latreasa was having difficulty focusing. There were no reported behavioral problems, but at school, her teacher shared that Latreasa would be easily distracted. If she saw a butterfly at the classroom window, she would jump up and just stare at it, exclaiming to all, how beautiful it was. When asked, the family indicated that these actions were being noticed after the tragic car accident in Chicago.

I know that God does not make mistakes. He told his disciples on at least one occasion to, "Let the children come." They were precious in the eyes of God and even angels were assigned to guard over them. Then one late afternoon, Latreasa had seen some silica sand, which had spilled off a box car on a set of railroad tracks near her home. She was bending over, scooping the same into a can when she was struck by a moving rail car and immediately killed. The train men had not seen the little girl and had released the car down the track. They were devastated, as were family members, when they rush to the scene of the accident. The community, church family, and everyone felt the horrific pain of the tragedy. I still shed a tear when I think of this dear little girl who had clung to me every Sunday morning.

Latreasa's funeral service was a somber experience for everyone. The family returned from the grave site for a quiet meal with a large number of family and friends at the church. As most people were finishing their meal, I noticed that Mary had gotten up and was walking toward the sanctuary. Onda and I both followed her and joined her at the altar rail. Kneeling there, we put our arms around her. She then asked us if we could say a special prayer for someone. She said, "Wade, there was a young man who was there with Latreasa after she was hit by the rail car, an ambulance attendant, and was so kind. He was so upset, and I can't get his face out of my mind." So, there on our knees, we prayed for this young man and all the kind people who reached out to the family during this tragic time.

After the family left the church and the wonderful people who prepared the meal were thanked, Onda and I left to run some errands before going home. We stopped first at JC Penny's to pick up a suit that was being altered. It was there in the men's department that I heard my name being called. I turned to find our young friend from Sunday school past, Frank Burger. Frank said, "Wade, I am so glad that I ran into you. I really need you to pray for someone. I was at the scene of a horrible train accident the other day. I don't know if you saw it in the paper, but a little girl was struck by a rail car and killed. I was on call for the ambulance service I work on and I still hurt for her mother and family."

"Frank," I said, "This little girl's mother just asked Onda and me to pray for you." Again, timing. Our timing, God's timing, they come together. She talked of this kind young man who was so upset over her daughter's death and wanted you to be comforted." I then shared with him on how we found her family in downtown Chicago in the midst of a crowd at a zoo. We rejoiced over how God had raised her up and how precious it was to baptize her and take "the plunge together." We marveled together on how in the midst of such a series of tragic events, God was making Himself known. He had promised that He would go through life's trials with us and He came through.

To this day, every time I hear the old church hymn, "Precious Memories," I cannot help but remember loved ones who've gone on to be with the Lord. People like mine and Onda's parents, grandparents, family members, and many friends. I especially remember this little girl named, Latreasa, for when the Lord Jesus said, "Let the little children come to me," she ran and jumped into His arms.

Chapter Seven

"SO YOU BELIEVE IN GOD!"

"You believe in God, even the demons believe and
they tremble in fear..."
James 2:19 RSV

There was a sense of urgency as I rushed to the hospital to meet a member of my congregation who had called stating that her husband had just had a massive heart attack and was in the intensive care unit. When I arrived, Ruth met me in the waiting room in tears. She said the doctors were not sure he would make it, but she was equally concerned that her husband, James, was not a Christian.

As I approached James' bedside, he recognized me and tried to be warm even though he was extremely weak. He told me that his doctors were not particularly encouraging, and that the prognosis was kind of bleak. He was without a doubt afraid and grasped my hand as I leaned over to tell him, "We love you James and the Lord loves you too." James replied, "I believe there is a God." I responded by saying, "James, even demons believe that there is a God and they tremble in fear." I am here to tell you that Jesus Christ is the Son of the Living God and that He not only loves you but wants to make His presence known to you. He wants to comfort you and assure you of His concern for your life and your soul."

James listened quietly as I and his wife shared for a few minutes how we had a personal relationship with Christ and the fact that there were many times we felt that He had rescued us from many trials in life. When I asked James if I could pray for him before I left his room, he immediately replied, "Please!" I assured him that I would check back on him for now he needed rest. I gave James a little cross pointing out that it said, "God Loves You." He was looking at it as I walked out of his room.

The very next morning, Ruth called Onda and said that James had another heart attack. "Please have Wade come quickly! James is dying!" This time, Ruth met me just outside his room crying, "You've got to save James. He told me to, call that preacher.'" He even went so far to say that he had seen and felt the fires of hell and that his, "feet and legs were burning up." I told Ruth, "I can't save anyone but we both know the One who can."

At his bedside, a very weak James had tears in his eyes as he explained that he felt so convicted of his sins he had committed in his life that he wanted me to say a prayer that the fires he was experiencing would go away. When I asked if he had prayed and asked God for help, he said that Ruth had prayed for him and that he felt a little better, but that now he wanted to make things right with the Lord.

This time, I reminded him of the things we had talked about earlier and how much God loved him. He was looking right into my eyes as I told him that Jesus wanted to forgive him and that He also wanted him to acknowledge Him as Savior. James was sobbing as he replied that he wanted forgiveness and Jesus in his life. In a matter of just a few moments, James confessed to us and to God, that he truly repented of his sins and now wanted Jesus to come into his heart. There was truly a look of peace on James' face as he kept saying, "Thank you, Lord! Thank you, Lord!"

With tears in her eyes, Ruth shared that Christ had truly answered her prayers for her husband. But now she pointed out that James had not been baptized. I told her that this was not a problem and I turned to James and asked if he now wanted to be baptized in this new faith that he had just confessed. Without hesitation, he replied, "Oh, yes, I do." With water drawn from a nearby faucet, James received holy baptism.

Now Ruth and James were both crying and laughing. They each shared their love for each other and how now they shared a mutual love of the Lord. Ruth turned to me and thanked me as if to say, all is complete now. Thinking I would be leaving, I told them, "The Holy Spirit is not done yet." I explained that I would like to anoint James with oil and pray that his affliction was not unto death, but that God would heal him. They both replied that additional prayers for James' recovery would be much appreciated. All three of us were crying as I anointed James with the oil I carried with me and I called upon the grace of the Lord and the name, Jesus, to heal him.

I returned to James' hospital room the very next afternoon and found him sitting in a chair. As I approached him, he said, "Wade, stand right there!" He arose out of his chair, took about two steps, and gave me a bear hug. He had difficulty speaking at that moment, but Ruth spoke up, saying that James' doctor and the nurses were confounded by his obvious improvement. He was still a little weak but the changes in his health in just a few hours were being described as nothing less than "miraculous."

About two weeks later following James' hospitalization for the heart attack, both he and Ruth showed up for church worship services. In the months to come, with the exception of icy roads during winter, they were there every Sunday. I asked Ruth how she felt now since God had answered her prayers. She replied that it was great except for one thing. When I asked what that could possibly be, she informed me that James watched Christian television continuously, day and night. Because he was hard of hearing James had the TV volume way up and often kept her awake at night.

James passed away almost one year to the day of his heart attack. His demeanor was never the same after his commitment to Christ. He radiated peace and he had some, boldness, as he talked of his faith. He held on to the little cross in his pocket up until he died. I am not sure it was the same cross I first gave him for I recall him occasionally asking for an extra cross. He never said why, or did I ever ask him what the extra crosses were for. I suspect that James was a servant-witness for the Lord, and he was checking out the heart monitors of others as well.

There was no question of what one of the hymns would be at his celebration service the day of his burial.

"Amazing Grace!"

AMAZING GRACE! HOW SWEET THE SOUND – THAT SAVED A WRETCH LIKE ME! I ONCE WAS LOST BUT NOW AM FOUND, WAS BLIND BUT NOW I SEE. TWAS GRACE THAT TAUGHT MY HEART TO FEAR, AND GRACE MY FEARS RELIEVED; HOW PRECIOUS DID THAT GRACE APPEAR THE HOUR I FIRST BELIEVED!

JOHN NEWTON

Note: God does not always answer prayer requests in the same manner. There is no doubt however, that God hears the prayers of faith and moves his hands according to His perfect will. In James' case, his wife had been praying for him for years. The church had prayed for him also and was there for James and Ruth to the very end.

Chapter Eight

"LYING DOWN ON THE JOB"

"My grace is sufficient for you, for my power is made
perfect in weakness...for when I am weak,then I am
strong"
2 Cor. 12:9-10 NIV

There are many Christians that believe God wants to use us according to His purpose, but then tend to think that those occasions will be the times we are on some "spiritual high" or perhaps following some Godly revelation. The truth is that this is not necessarily the case for a servant is on call regardless of whether or not he or she are at their very best. God may wish to use us even when we may feel that we are at our weakest, physically, emotionally, or spiritually. I discovered a long time ago that it was not my timing or agenda that the Lord was interested in. It was my being obedient and realizing that God has us always on "standby." I learned that in the time when I was ill, or feeling extremely weak, that I would not be granted a leave of absence.

Several years ago, I was committed to going on a mission trip to Africa. I had been an emergency medical technician and had served on an all-volunteer ambulance service for over eight years. I was being given the opportunity to work in a small hospital at a mission site which served the spiritual and physical needs of hundreds of people. Even though I had no known medical problems, it was a matter of common sense that I had a physical exam before I would leave the country. While the blood work showed no problems, it was during the exam that I shared with my doctor that I had occasional discomfort in my throat. My very alert doctor and friend felt that this was suspicious and ordered a thallium X-Ray. This test showed possible blockages in my heart.

Instead of packing for Africa, I was instead scheduled for a heart Cath known as an angiography. I was wheeled into a heart Cath lab where I was met by a great team of medical technicians who were caring and very professional. Before the exam, it was explained that there were risks as with any surgical procedure. I felt assured and told them that if anything went sour that I was under the care of a wonderful Cardiologist and my Heavenly Doctor was assisting. The procedure went fine, and some blockages were successfully ballooned to provide better blood circulation. It was incredible to experience such peace through the treatment and afterward.

I was particularly drawn to a tall medical assistant named, Stephen. He remained with me following the procedure to put pressure on the entry point of the catheter for several minutes to prevent bleeding. It was during this time that Stephan wanted to know what I had meant about not being afraid and my reference to a Heavenly Doctor. He explained that he was having difficulty with "faith in God." He said that he had seen so much human suffering and could not understand that if there was a loving God, how could He allow so much pain and suffering. I told my new young friend that I could share what I learned in seminary for his question was as old as the ages, or that I could share my own experiences. He quickly replied that he wanted to hear how I came to understand this and if there was such a thing as having a personal relationship with the God of creation.

I might have been a little "out of it" from the drugs administered before and during the heart Cath, but I wanted to tell him about the Lord Jesus. I found myself telling him the story of Latreasa whom I had written about earlier. I shared that God had not appeared to have intervened to prevent the crisis this little girl had experienced, but that God was with her all the time. I pointed out that even though her death was tragic, it was evident that God was making Himself known and that He would never leave us or forsake us. This is hard to understand, I said, but that our faith is built on trust and love. I explained that had I died during the surgery, God had not abandoned me for I felt His presence and especially His peace.

Stephen admitted that he wanted to hear more and understand. I asked, if he had a chance, I hoped he could come by my room later that I had something to give him. The very next morning, Stephen came by my room and we had a brief follow-up conversation. Before he left, I told him, "God loves you and I love you. I appreciate your kindness and you are definitely being called to a ministry of caring." With this I gave him the "little cross in my pocket" and told him I would pray that Jesus would manifest Himself and reveal to him His plan for his life.

It was over a year later that I heard from Stephen. I had told Onda about this young man that appeared to me like an angel and we should pray for him. We were both surprised and concerned when Onda began experiencing chest pains. Our doctor did not hesitate and referred her to my cardiologist, who scheduled her for a heart Cath.

Onda said later that she had remembered my description of Stephen, but in the Cath Lab, all the technicians had surgical masks on. She asked if any of them knew Stephen, who had worked in the lab. All of a sudden, a tall, young man stepped forward. He looked a little startled even behind the mask when he said he was Stephen. Onda then told him that he possibly did not remember her husband, Wade, but that he had given him a little cross. Stephen said, "I remember Wade!" With this he reached beneath his lab shirt and pulled out the little cross that says, "God Love You." He had drilled a little hole in it and had put it on a chain. He told Onda that he wore the cross every day and that I should tell Wade that things were going well for him.

He said he is still learning about God's love and a little more about His plan for his life.

As Paul wrote to the Corinth church, "God's grace is sufficient!" (2Cor12:9NIV) His power is perfected through our faith and obedience even when we are weak and feel that we are laying down on the job. I found this to be so true as I continued to make a number of trips to the hospital as a patient in the years to come.

On one occasion, I had to be transported from one hospital to another some thirty miles away to have a stent placed in blocked artery. This time, I spent the whole trip ministering to a young woman who was going through a divorce. I wasn't really at my best but this EMT was hurting more than I was in many ways. I managed to share with her that divorce is serious business to God and He is serious in helping her. I could only tell her that God loved her and her estranged husband. I was unable to give her a cross, but she said talking really helped. She was open to counseling and hopefully to Godly advice. I think I felt a little like an exhausted Dr. Kildare by the time we arrived at the hospital. I know the Lord Jesus makes house and hospital calls, but I was still on call as I would soon learn.

The implanted stent went well and after a reunion with old friends in the Cath Lab, I was placed in a two-patient room. That evening, another patient was admitted and now occupied the other bed. I really felt bad that he was having some discomfort for he kept moaning. Finally, it looked like neither one of us was going to get any sleep, so I got out of bed and walked to his side. I told him that I had just underwent a procedure and that I felt confident that what was done for me would promote healing and that he too should be hopeful. He replied that he was having some discomfort but that he was afraid of what was happening to him. I quietly told him that I understood and as a pastor I had prayed for many people in similar circumstances. I asked him if he would like for me to pray for him. He said, "I sure would like prayer." I don't remember what I prayed but before I got back into my bed, he was snoring. And he snored and he snored. I didn't get a lot of sleep that night, but he did.

Early the next morning, he was taken to the Cath Lab. Onda had arrived shortly thereafter to take me home. She had one of our little crosses with her so I placed it on his nightstand with a note saying that I would remember him in prayer. I also prayed quietly that he would be totally healed.

Jesus must love visiting the hospital. Over the years, I have felt His presence in the halls and patient rooms. I have felt Him even when I was "lying down on the job" feeling pretty weak. I'm always telling doctors, nurses, and medical personnel that;

"God sure makes you folks look real good!" And He gets all the glory! Amen!

Chapter Nine

"THERE'S SOMETHING ABOUT THAT NAME!"

"Blessed be His name forever; may the whole earth be
filled with His glory."
Ps 72:19 NIV

The name, "JESUS!" There is something wonderful about that Name. For Christians, the name of our Savior means love and grace. The name, Jesus, invokes comfort and healing. It is mentioned in reverence and denotes a personal relationship which is alive with devotion and commitment. When the world uses His name or the name of the Father in an irreverent manner, it causes pain in the heart of those who believe in the cross of Christ and His saving grace. To call upon the name of Jesus is a great privilege that is a gift of the Holy Spirit which resides in the hearts of the children of God. The name is to be revered in worship and lifted up in our petitions.

On one occasion, Onda and I had to pick up our daughter, Tami, and son, Everett, both in their teens at the time, before we could attend a prayer meeting with close Christian friends. Our kids were attending a "Right to Life" meeting where our daughter was secretary.

We had just started up a narrow road on a sharp curve when we saw a car headed toward us at a very high speed. The sparks were flying as the car scraped the guard rail on one side of the road and then the other as the driver swerved to regain control. It was now in our lane of traffic and was headed right toward us. We were within seconds of a collision and there was no shoulder to pull off the road. In a voice above a whisper, Onda called out, "Jesus! Help!"

Somehow, I managed to come to a screeching halt and had just put the car in reverse. The oncoming car swerved just a little, but still struck the left front of our vehicle, throwing us forward with a tremendous jolt. Somehow, we were not injured, and I managed to jump out of our car and run after the other vehicle as it was not stopping but was still rolling.

I was able to reach through the driver's window and pull the gear shift up to park. I then turned the engine off and realized that the driver was trying to reposition himself in the seat to restart the car to possibly drive away. There was a horrific smell of alcohol as he yelled, "Who in the (expletive) are you!?" He was cursing me and God as I showed him my badge. I was asking if he was injured just as a police car with emergency lights on came around the curve and stopped. The police officer recognized me and stated that he had clocked this car on radar at speeds over eighty miles an hour and was in pursuit. He expressed surprise that neither Onda nor I were seriously injured. The driver of the speeding car appeared not be injured and was placed under arrest for driving while intoxicated. Onda and I would have to remain at the accident scene to provide additional information.

Onda was still sitting in the car, softly saying, "Thank you Jesus!" She insisted that she was not hurt but shaken up. Her attention immediately turned to the fact that our children would be waiting for us to pick them up. Onda again said, "Lord, we need some help here."

At that very moment, a car pulled up behind us and our friends, Bill and Sharon Pfeiffer, seeing that we were involved in a head on collision, ran up to us. The Pfeiffer's were part of our prayer group and would have seen us later at our prayer meeting. They agreed to pick up the children and would explain to them that we were involved in a car accident and assure them that we were not injured. Before they left, we had a little praise, appreciation moment, thanking God.

We were late to our meeting but rejoiced that we got there at all. The car had severe damage to the front end but was drivable and could be repaired. Bill and Sharon had delivered our kids home and had shared with our many friends what had happened. Later that evening, Bill said he still couldn't explain why he took that particular road of our accident since it was not on a direct route to the meeting.

Our evening gathering was filled with praise, worship, study, and prayer. We shared our gratitude to the Lord for we could have been killed in a car accident. There were others who had thanksgivings but also several needs were shared and needed prayed. Our dear friend, Loraine Shelton, prayed for her husband, Jim, who had shown an interest in the faith, but had remained skeptical. Others had similar needs and Onda and I prayed that the name of Jesus would receive glory for all that He had done and was doing.

The very next day, I made arrangements for our car to be repaired and stopped by police headquarters to pick up a copy of our accident report. It turned out that the driver had tested way over the legal limit of intoxication and was also charged with having no valid Driver's License. He had been arrested prior for DWI and had lost his license. The report also showed that the actual owner of the car was the father of the driver.

A couple of nights later, I called the owner to see if he had any car insurance. The father of the driver was cordial and apologetic. He stated that his son had taken his car without his permission. He also shared that his son had a severe drinking problem and had several encounters with law enforcement. I told the man that my wife and I were grateful that no one was injured and that we had prayed for his son the night of the accident. I made it clear that while his son had to "face the music", we still had no ill feelings toward him. In fact, we felt a little sorry for the depth of this man's addiction to alcohol and hoped that he could be healed. Right after I said this, the man said, "You're Butch, aren't you?" Taken somewhat aback, I admitted that my nickname was "Butch," and that only family and close friends knew that. When I inquired how he knew my nickname, he replied, "Butch, I work for Jim Shelton," Loraine's husband. We had just prayed for Jim the night of our car accident. We had asked the Lord that Jim would experience an understanding of Christ's love and now he was in some way linked to our car accident.

We would later call our accident, "A God Incident," for there were more than coincidences happening here. The very next evening, Jim called to say that he heard all about our accident. First, from his wife, Loraine and then from his employee, who was the father of the other driver of the car. He asked me about the conversation that I had with the father of the driver. He admitted that had it been him involved in such an accident, he would have been upset, more likely even furious. Jim wanted to know why we did not express anger over the incident. I shared how Onda had called on the name, "Jesus!" And that we felt His presence throughout the whole incident, for there was peace and we were filled with thanksgiving. Onda and I were grateful that no one was injured when it was possible that we all might have been killed. Jim listened patiently and agreed that if I got him a little pocket cross that he would give it to his worker, who in turn would give it to his son.

We were saddened to hear some time later that the young man had died and we never had any more contact with him or his father. Jim, on the other hand, did later give his heart to Christ and we rejoiced with Loraine for her prayers were answered. Again, we continue to marvel at another "God incident" for all the events from that night were not just coincidence but a part of God's divine will. Onda agreed that our accident was part of a divine plan, but hoped the next time, and hopefully there would be no next time, that it would not be her car that we might be driving but my car with all the police radios in it. It was safely sitting in the garage the night of the accident.

TAKE THE NAME OF JESUS WITH YOU

Take the name of Jesus with you, Child of sorrow and of woe. It will joy and comfort give you, Take it then wher-e'er you go. Take the name of Jesus ever As protection every – where; If temptations 'round you gather, Breathe that ho–ly name in prayer. Precious name, O how sweet! Hope of earth and joy of heaven. Precious name, O how sweet! Hope of earth and joy of heaven.

Lydia Baxter

Chapter Ten

"THE GIFT THAT KEEPS ON GIVING"

"I long to see you so that I may impart to you some
spiritual gift to make you strong – that is, that you and
I may be mutually encouraged by each other's faith."
Romans 1:11 NIV

While the call that God places on our hearts is
unending to be a servant -witness, our ministry to
others in sharing God's love is not a one-way street. Paul
wrote in his letters to the churches how he was encouraged by the faith and support of others. He spoke of how
co-workers like Luke, Timothy, Silas, Titus, and many
others were a constant blessing to him. And then there were
the new Christians that he had led to Christ that were in
turn providing comfort and support. The establishment
of Christian churches has brought forth the concept of

community, a people of faith who are called, "The Family of God."

Over the years, so many of those whom we reached out to in love, have in turn so often reached out to Onda and I in ways that we will forever be grateful. These were Christian brothers and sisters who saw or felt our need for support or encouragement. Many of whom we had only little contact and yet they reached out to us. There were many people who came back into our lives years later. These moments were and continue to be a tremendous blessing to us.

One such contact was a young man that I had worked with a few years earlier. Ken had been a troubled teenager and difficult to work with. He was constantly getting into trouble at school and also with local police authorities. He was a likable kid, but to be honest, I would have liked to spank him (in love, of course) at times for the ridiculous situations he got himself into. After one such incident, I had to send him back to a juvenile detention facility for a criminal offense that could be described as just plain stupid. He did return to society after a brief detention period and after several months of patient supervision, did earn a discharge from parole. During that time, there were some spiritual conversations that showed a lot of maturity and I think I had given him a little pocket cross as he was presented with his discharge.

A few years later and short time after entering the ministry, I was having a little self-pity party over the fact that I was unsure of what I had really accomplished with my life. I was in the process of complaining to Onda about our transition to the pastorate and my doubts concerning my life accomplishments. We were sitting at the dining room table at about nine o'clock at night when the phone rang. One could imagine my surprised when I picked up the phone and the voice on the other line identified himself as Ken.

Ken stated that he was now living in Florida and had been thinking of me. He recalled how I had been so patient when he was younger and doing some "pretty dumb things." He went on to say that he was married and just had a baby boy born, who he had named, "Wade." The voice on the other end sounded so mature as he went on to say that God had placed it on his heart to call and tell me that he had remembered the things that I had shared with him and that he and his wife were Christians and attending church. I had a little difficulty clearing my throat to thank Ken for his call. Before we hung up, I asked him how he was able to find me since I had moved to another part of the state. He said an operator had taken time to do something, which made the phone connection possible. I would have liked to talk to that operator.

After we hung up, I didn't feel any self-pity, but I sure was embarrassed. As I told Onda of Ken and my conversation, I tried also to apologize to her for being kind of childish and complaining but she interrupted saying, "I tried to tell you so." I had tried to put my previous life's work under a microscope and had forgotten that I was on deployment for the Lord that whole time and that the mission was for His purpose, not mine.

This incident brought to my mind that on another occasion I was talking to an elderly black grandmother about her grandson's pending parole when she stopped to ask, "Mr. Gregory, how are you feeling?" I was a little taken aback but I remember unloading somewhat by saying I was so tired. I had been so busy that I was feeling a little overwhelmed. Almost instantly, this large woman jumps out of her seat and picks me up out my chair. She lifted me up into the air, hugging me the whole time. Before she put me back on my feet, she says with tears in her eyes, "Honey child! Don't you know you are on the Lord's time?" These remembrances, along with Ken's phone call, are trips down memory lane that are gifts that keep on giving. I don't feel sorry for myself anymore. I see myself as a Christian under construction that is wholly dependent upon the grace of Christ and the support of those around me, the family of God.

Even in the time of personal loss, I have been reminded of how important it is to lean on Christ and others for support. When my mother died, I was faced with her passing and my upcoming heart surgery. Needless to say, my strength was at a low point. At the funeral visitation, a young man approached Onda and I immediately felt a surge of renewed energy and strength. Here was a young man from my past who had an extremely difficult life. Danny had a horrible habit of making bad mistakes. While likable, he had been very insecure, and his younger years were filled with family problems that led to a severe acting out problem. He was rebellious but inside was tender and at times, self-destructive.

On one occasion, Danny was arrested for a crime he was not really guilty of and I was prepared to go to court and testify on his behalf. A couple of days before the trial, I received an urgent message to come to the sheriff's office via my police radio. When I arrived, I found Danny in the hallway almost sobbing. Finding a vacant office, I took Danny aside to privately find out what was going on. He slumped down in a chair and showed me his wrist. He had been holding a blood-soaked handkerchief over an apparent wound. Danny then admitted that he wanted to kill himself and had cut his wrist. He went on to say that he couldn't stand the thought that if he went to court, he might be sent to an adult prison facility for a crime he didn't commit. I immediately thought, "Been there! Done this before! Lord, I need a little help here!"

When I asked Danny what he had been doing to his wrist, he pulled out a pocketknife with blood on it. I found myself telling Danny that this definitely was not the plan that God had for his life. I pointed out that God truly loved him and has been trying to rescue him for some time. This time was no exception and that he should not give into hopelessness for he was not alone. I, for one, would be there for him. I then told him that he did not have to give me the knife, but would he trade it for a little cross that I held in my hand that says, "God Loves You!" Danny took the little cross and after looking at it for a few minutes, handed me the knife.

The story for Danny did end well. In court, I, as well as a police detective testified on his behalf. The charge was dismissed, and Danny made a lot of progress in the next few months. It was a joyous day for both of us when I handed him his discharge papers from parole. I kept the pocket-knife and have used it as a letter opener.

And here was Danny, at the funeral home visitation years later to share his condolences over my mother's death. He wore that same smile that I remembered. He first approached Onda, who recognized him, and turned to me and said, "Danny is here." He shared with us that he had seen the notice of mother's death in the newspaper and that he wanted to express his sorrow for our loss. He then added that he wanted me to know that he was now married and had children of his own. He also shared that he had become a "born again Christian" and had joined a Christian band, which had a tremendous effect on his life. He was involved in a jail ministry and wanted me to know how his life had changed. God had truly delivered Danny from a tumultuous past and he acknowledged that he was blessed to have a Christian wife and family.

Danny's sharing with me truly lifted me from severe weakness to feeling a joy that produced strength and a sense of victory. Danny was a gift to me, as was Ken. I will be eternally grateful for these are gifts that remind me of God's love and the gift of salvation. His gift of love and grace keeps on giving. John, "The Apostle of Love," wrote these words to remind and encourage the Family of God, "and God himself has said that one must not only love God, but his brother (and sisters) too. (1John 4:32)

Chapter Eleven

"THE LORD MUST HAVE A SENSE OF HUMOR"

"There is a time for everything, and a season for every
activity under heaven...a time to weap and a time to
laugh, a time to mourn and a time to dance."
Ec. 3:1, 4 NIV

It should come as no surprise that God's business is serious
business. There is nothing more important than having
a personal relationship with the Lord Jesus. The call that
God places on the hearts of his disciples is to be a servant
and witness of his love and grace is very "serious business."
On the other hand, it is good to remember that Jesus said,
"I have come that you may have and enjoy life, and have it
in abundance, till it overflows." (John 10:10b Amplified
Bible) He then added that he loved his friends and told us

all that "My joy be in you and that your joy may be complete" (John15:11)

Jesus stressed that this is serious business but made it clear that his joy comes as a gift to encourage us and to put a smile on our face, not a frown. He taught us to focus on our mission but also to be able to laugh and enjoy the fullness of all that our heavenly father has given us. With his eyes on the upcoming cross, his heart was full of joy as he saw the faces of small children who wanted to crawl upon his lap, the expressions of wonder as he worked miracles among the crowds of people, and a sense of hope being restored to the multitudes of people who had little or no hope.

This gift often comes as healing after a "sick, sad, and sorry" event in our lives. To know Christ is to know a humor that embraces us when He lifts us out of a bad situation. To look upon Christ is to see our Savior with a smile upon his face. To know that when we laugh while watching children at play or even little animals wrestling with one another, God is laughing too. He has a sense of humor and when he wipes our tears from our eyes, we laugh with him because of the fullness of his joy that he has gifted us.

We all tend to perceive things that happen mostly through our own experiences. In other words, our understanding of life comes from the experiences we have in living our life. When Christ is in us, we are to see life as Christ is revealing it to us through His eyes. As we grow in Christ, we have the opportunity to see things from God's point of view. When we are young, we see things as a child. As we mature, our understanding of life experiences takes on a whole new perspective.

As an example, one day our five-year-old great-grandson, Andrew, called his grandmother to tell her about his visit to the Indianapolis Children's Museum. When asked what he saw, he excitedly said he saw "Three mommies all wrapped up in toilet paper and wet wipes." This evidently satisfied him on what he saw and how he understood the Egyptian exhibit at the museum.

Our family had a good laugh at Andrew's explanation of a life experience, but we did not laugh at him. Neither does God laugh at us in our youthful understanding. But I believe God does have a sense of humor and a room filled with laughter in the joy of the Lord is like a sanctuary filled with worship praise to the Lord.

Onda and I have found that the opportunity to share Christ's love in giving a person a little pocket cross has often come with times of humor as well as times wrought with sadness or even with tears.

On one such occasion, Onda and I had a chance encounter with an old friend who had been a fellow police officer. Scotty was an outgoing man who was quick to display a temper, but we loved him. During our visit with him, he admitted that he had a problem of getting angry though his emotions only lasted for a short time. He shared with Onda that he wished he could control such outbursts. Onda said little except, "God loves you Scotty, and you undoubtedly know that He doesn't like his name taken in vain." With this, she smiled as she gave him a little cross and he thanked her as he put it in his pocket.

We had not seen Scotty again for a few weeks but when we ran into him one day, he walked up to us with a smile on his face. He asked Onda if she remembered the little cross, she had given. She replied, "Of course I do." Scotty then went on to tell us that whenever he got mad, he always had a habit of jamming his fist into his pants pocket. He was laughing with tears in his eyes as he explained that after a few "mad fits" and jamming his fist into his pocket that he had cut himself on the edge of the little cross. "At first," he said, "I wanted to take the cross out of my pocket for good, but each time, I did, I saw the words on the cross which says, 'God Loves You.'" Scotty was laughing as were we when he added, "I finally decided that how could God possibly love me when I fly into a rage and say things I really don't mean." He went on to say, "I don't do that anymore. Each time I think I will get mad I don't dare for that little cross cuts into my heart when I even think about it. I'll always keep it in my pocket to remind me that I don't have to get mad." By this time, all three of us had little tears of joy in our eyes. Scotty had a new life experience, which brought him new understanding of God's love and grace. I believe God must have a sense of humor and was laughing with us.

Laughter can promote healing and is often contagious. Onda and I have found our days full of joy because we are so grateful to the Lord for all he has done for us and others around us. He has done wondrous things for us, with us, through us, and at times, in spite of us. "The joy of the Lord is truly our strength" (Neh 8:10) and while we take God's business seriously, we try to not take ourselves too seriously. Without a doubt, laughter and joy has promoted healing in our lives and the lives of others.

Some years ago, I had open heart surgery and the operation along with a lot of prayer likely saved my life. I was in the hospital with all kinds of tubes and wires running in and out of my body. For some reason, the heart monitor there at my bedside did not bother me for I had peace as I remembered all those hours at my grandfather's side at the hospital years earlier. Anyway, in walked Onda's and mine dear Christian friends, Joe and Lois Eakle. Joe hits the door and says, "Wade, are you going to be wimp about this or what? God isn't done with you yet!" We all laughed, especially me who probably had a little more pain because of the exertion. I know the prayer they said before they left was comforting and I felt better. The laughter that day has lasted all these years and remains a part of my healing experience.

Then there was the time I was leading the pallbearers to a graveside to conduct final services for a church member and friend. I had grown close to this gentleman for I had been with him throughout his illness. I had given him a cross in the hospital following a serious heart attack and now a year later we were there to say goodbye for at least a little while. Stepping up to lift the casket onto the grave rollers, one man at the front end of the casket put his foot down on the green carpet a little too close to the grave hole and his left leg immediately sank down to his hip. Both I and the funeral director rushed to help the man pull his leg out of the grave and place the casket onto the rollers. I then, without thinking, said, "Fellow, you had better be careful! You've already got one foot in the grave."

Unfortunately, all of the pallbearers, including myself and the funeral director, started laughing just as the family of the deceased walked up to be seated under the family tent. As I attempted to apologize and explain what had happened, everyone started laughing, including the family members. One of the man's sons said, "Dad would have loved this!" Then for several minutes, family members and friends shared funny stories that spoke of the deceased with much affection and love. It became evident that this time of sharing became part of the healing process. The death of a Christian will bring forth sadness for family and friends alike but the promise of hope of life eternal, and a joy that fills our heart with thanksgiving and praise is a precious gift. We were able to close this chapter of a man's life, giving the Lord our love and appreciation for a life well lived.

There have been so many occasions when the spirit of peace and comfort was present with such power that tears were turned to smiles and even laughter. God does have a sense of humor which will shine through to all us.

There is a familiar church hymn, "In the Garden," whose chorus has touched many lives for almost a century:

"AND HE WALKS WITH ME, AND HE TALKS WITH ME, AND HE TELLS ME I AM HIS OWN, AND THE JOY WE SHARE AS WE TARRY THERE, NONE OTHER HAS EVER KNOWN."

C. Austin Miles, 1912 Hall Mack Co.

Chapter Twelve

"THE PERFECT WEDDING GIFT"

"On the first day, a wedding took place at Cana in
Galilee. Jesus' mother was there, and his disciples had
also been invited."
John 2:1 – 2 NIV

The air was so dense you could cut it with a knife as
I walked into the church that Saturday afternoon. A
young couple was to be married and their families were
making final preparations for the ceremony. The wedding
rehearsal had went with little difficulty the previous evening but it was evident that something was amiss. In the
"old days," some would have called this a "shotgun wedding"
but in meetings with this young man and woman, both in
their teens, it was clear that they loved each other and
wanted a Christian wedding as they started their family.

Unfortunately, the couple's parents were not talking to each other and there were unresolved feelings over the circumstances surrounding the marriage. One could sense the disappointment in the couple as I talked to them separately, but they were excited about their wedding and were trying to make the best of the situation. The bride, in her white gown looked radiant and the groom in another area of the church was nervous but anxious to start the service. Even the best man and the groomsmen felt the same way.

After a little reflection and a little prayer for guidance I went back to the couple separately and asked if it would be alright to have Holy Communion as part of their service. I planned a devotion time in the service but somehow, there had to be ways to minister to the whole family and at the same time celebrate the occasion with joy and enthusiasm. In separate conversations with the two youngsters, they both agreed with surprising excitement, even with such a late suggestion.

I was still not sure if I was listening to answered prayer as I called Onda before she arrived at the church if she could prepare the elements for an unplanned communion service. We had a few minutes and somehow Onda, almost miraculously, had a small load of bread and grape juice for the communion chalice ready.

By this time I was a little nervous. I couldn't help but think how the bride might feel if she got grape stains all over her beautiful wedding gown. And besides that, the air was still a little blue, but after the presentation of the bride by her father and gathered now at the altar, there was a wonderful peace.

For the now unprepared devotion, I found myself sharing the story of Jesus at the wedding in the little town of Cana and how quietly he and the disciples were as they witnessed the ceremony and the celebration afterwards. To think that the Son of God was present at the wedding and how the guests were probably completely unaware of his presence. But Jesus' mother knew he was there, and she learned, most likely from just a few of the close family members, that the gathering was running out of wine for all the guests. Mary didn't know what Jesus would do but she knew this family was faced with embarrassment and the wedding celebration might come to an abrupt end and the family would possibly be faced with humiliation. Jesus briefly protested to his mother that this was not the time to bring attention to His power, but out of immense love for His mother and her wishes, He tells the stewards of the feast to fill ceremonial jars with water. After they comply, He told them to pour some of the contents into a cup and take it to the master of the banquet. They did as directed and when the master of ceremonies tasted the water turned to wine, he exclaims how this wine was the best and compliments the bridegroom's family of the wonderful quality of the wine and the fact that he saved the best for the last.

The miracle at Cana (John 2:1-11NIV), I explained, was the best wedding gift of all. The one gift that every couple should hope for, to even pray for, the gift was in the person of Christ, present and manifesting His love for people. The blessing upon the institution of marriage, ordained by our heavenly Father, was Him showing His love for the family. The Lord wants to save us from the humiliation of our failings and save us all from being embarrassed. I added that we would celebrate this love in remembrance at the Lord's Table and that this young couple wanted their family and friends to be aware that they wanted to establish their home in this love.

Following the exchange of vows and the consecration of the elements, the wedding couple very sweetly shared in the breaking of bread and took of the cup. They eagerly agreed to now share in the communion by holding the cup and the bread. I made sure that the groom took the cup to be shared.

Then the miracle of Cana once again occurred. The two families responded by getting up from their seats, but before coming to the altar, were embracing one another. Nothing was being said but it was obvious that much healing was being experienced. Most of the family and friends now came to the altar and the young couple was happy to greet their loved ones as ministers of their own celebration.

What a joy to present their wedding certificate and the two little crosses, that says, "God Loves You!" The best wedding gift of all, however, was the fact that Jesus showed up and manifested His love and healing ways.

I have no way of remembering how many little pocket crosses shared with wedding couples but the number of miracles that I have seen are remarkable when Jesus becomes the center and focus of the marriage . When families invite Christ into their marriage, their home becomes a temple. Troubled water is turned into sweet wine and lives of all in the home are blessed.

The important thing is that when families, faced with brokenness, ask Christ to heal their brokenness, he can and will. I have even seen couples who were told to give up and not bother with further counseling by psychologists, are these who have often turned to the Lord and experienced healing. I have even seen these couples incorporated into the church and become leaders. In almost every case, those who have been rescued form the humiliation of broken marriages, even divorce have been able to minister to others going through the same pain. There have been many little crosses shared by those who have received the perfect wedding gift.

It should be noted that many times I have seen God work through problems in people's marriages or anything else for that matter. I have told these "blessed individuals" that God may well want to use them in the future for they will possibly come in contact with those going through the same kind of problem. This is often the case. The rescued become a vital part of God's Plan to rescue others. It is so often the case that people can believe the Lord can do things, even miracles in lives of others but can't accept the fact that our Loving Father can or will do things for them. Our faith is built on the promises of God. We have to believe that these are promises for us all.

As a child, I remembered the times my mother would play the piano, and my father, sister, Carla and I would gather around and sing our favorite hymn by Stuart Hamblen. I found myself using this hymn which I shared with those gathered at my sister's funeral service.

It Is No Secret

THE CHIMES OF TIME RING OUT THE NEWS;
ANOTHER DAY IS THROUGH.
SOMEONE SLIPPED AND FELL. WAS THAT
SOMEONE YOU? YOU MAY HAVE LONGED
FOR ADDED STRENGTH, YOUR COURAGE TO
RENEW. DO NOT BE DISHEARTENED, FOR I
BRING HOPE TO YOU.
IT IS NO SECRET WHAT GOD CAN DO. WHAT
HE'S DONE FOR OTHERS, HE'LL DO FOR YOU.
WITH ARMS WIDE OPEN, HE'LL PARDON YOU,
IT IS NO SECRET WHAT GOD CAN DO.

Stuart Hamblen

Chapter Thirteen

"FORGET THE CLOWNS! SEND IN THE CHEERLEADERS!"

"Therefore, since we are surrounded by such a great
cloud of witnesses, let us throw off everything that
hinders [us] ... and let us run with perseverance the
race marked out for us."
Hebrews 12:1 (NIV)

O ne of the responsibilities of being a grandparent is
attending your grandchildren's sporting events, school
programs, music recitals, etc. On one such occasion, Onda
and I attended one our grandson's little league baseball game.
Gabrien had progressed past T-Ball and was playing right field
for his team. A batter on the opposing team came to bat and
on the first pitch, hit the ball and began running to first base.
He had made it safely but instead of stopping or going on to
second base, this young lad kept on running out into right

field. His coaches and teammates started yelling at him to stop, but he just kept on running. My grandson even put his arms out to stop him, but he ran past him and continued into the outfield. By now, coaches and members of both teams were running after him and many in the crowd stood and cheered. Some yelled, "Stop! You are going the wrong way!" I stood also and I couldn't help myself. I started yelling, "Run Forest! Run!"

By the time several players and coaches caught up with the young player, it appeared that there was some kind of celebration going on in deep right field. From the stands it was hard to see if the runner had thought that he had hit a home run or maybe even scored a touchdown. It was obvious that some of the coaches, teammates, and his parents were a little embarrassed. It must have been confusing to the little ball player however, as he got a standing ovation as he took a seat in the dugout.

One thing is for sure, this little league game was far more interesting and entertaining than any ball game I had ever seen. I remain convinced that this young lad has been coached better since and probably has not made the same mistake. Hopefully, there will be coaches, teammates, and yes, cheerleaders to train and to encourage him all his life.

There have been Christians that have made it to first base but have not made it to second base and certainly not to home plate. Christians have the best coach in the world. The Lord Jesus has sent his Holy Spirit to guide and direct us throughout our entire life. It is disappointing to say the least, that a Christian is not victorious when he or she has failed to follow Christ according to His word and divine direction. It is equally disappointing that sometimes the servant leaders have failed to be the shepherds that Christ has called them to be and the cheerleaders were not there to properly encourage and support the "runners of the race."

That is why Christ has called each Christian to be a servant-witness and share our faith with others. We are to live our lives to exemplify Christ and to lend our support so that all of us can make it to the winner's circle.

I remember well, a young lady figure skater in the winter Olympic Games some years ago had fallen down during the final competition. She quickly got to her feet and resumed her presentation to the roar of the crowd. Everyone in the ice rink was a cheerleader and she went on to win the gold. She made it to the winner's circle for the gold metal even though she had made a mistake. With a smile on her face, she had made such an impression on the judges and on the crowd that she surely was a winner.

I don't know about other Christians, but I know I have fallen a few times and there were cheerleaders encouraging me. I am eternally grateful that we all have a patient, loving coach to help us get to home plate. I haven't made it to the winner's circle yet, but the Bible says we even have a "cloud of witnesses" (Heb12:1NIV) rooting for us all. Truly, they can be called "Cheerleaders."

The times that I have shared with others and even gave a little cross that says, "God Loves You" has been in the role of a cheerleader. Years ago, a man called me before a Maundy Thursday service, the celebration at the Lord's Table, which honors the Lord's last meal before crucifixion. Aaron explained that he could not attend for he felt completely defeated and that God just was not there for him and his family. His infant son was ill and medical expenses had put him into a crisis situation, which he could not handle at all. At that late hour, there was nothing I could say to encourage him except that I understood his dilemma and concern. I had time to say that God would not abandon him, and then he hung up.

A short time later, I noticed Aaron sitting in the congregation alone in the darkened sanctuary during our communion service. He truly looked downtrodden when he came sheepishly forward to receive the holy elements. After the service, Onda and I joined Aaron, who was sitting in a pew at the back of the sanctuary. After a brief conversation, Onda whispered that we were to give him whatever we had to help him and his family. I replied that God had already made it clear that we were not only encourage him but give him whatever cash we had. I fumbled for my billfold and found twenty-five dollars. But before I could give it to Aaron, the Spirit was saying to me, "Check your coat pocket." I retrieved a quarter and gave Aaron all that we had with us. (Twenty-five dollars and twenty-five cents). Aaron was taken aback and said that he couldn't accept it and that he was so much deeper in debt. I explained to Aaron that he had to accept it for we were under orders. Aaron did look a little better and he thanks us before he left to return home where his wife was carrying for their ailing child.

It was almost midnight when Aaron called. When I answered, he was apparently crying and laughing at the same time. He went on to explain that when he got home, he sat at his desk and looked at some of the unopened bills. He was particularly concerned about the phone bill, which would soon be overdue. He was afraid that he would lose his phone service, and this would be horrible for he and his wife had to call for an ambulance on a couple of occasions when their son had a medical crisis. I had a little trouble understanding Aaron at first, but he finally blurted out that when he opened the phone bill, he found that his bill was exactly twenty-five dollars and twenty-five cents. I was shedding a few tears when Aaron proclaimed that God had not forgotten him and that he would someway make it. The Lord made it clear that he did love him, his family and ailing child.

Aaron did make it, but it wasn't easy. He found that he had several cheerleaders, his church, who were there also to lend a hand. He had not been abandoned and he learned that Christ didn't promise to take him right out of his seemly hopeless situation, but he did promise to go through it with him.

There is a secular song that says, "Send in the clowns" as if this might lift one out of a terrible situation, but the truth is, "sending in the cheerleaders" has more redemptive results. The coach is there to see us through to the winners' circle. This was what Paul was writing to the church in Rome, when he said that we were Christ's body of chosen people and that we understand who we are by knowing Him for whom He is and what He does for us. As part of His body, we run for Home Plate. He says, "Run for dear life and be alert servants of the Master." Then he added, "Be cheerfully expectant."

A Prayer

Loving Father,

Everything good comes from you. Everything happens
through you. Everything ends up in you so that you
always receive the Glory. Empower us so we can be the
cheerleaders that you called us to be and perform our
assigned tasks according to your Love, Joy and Grace.

WE ASK THIS IN JESUS NAME
AMEN

Chapter Fourteen

"Just Passing Through On My Way To New Jerusalem"

"I revealed myself to those who did not ask for; I was
found by those who did not seek...To a people that did
not call on my name, I said, 'Here I am!' "
Is 65:1 NIV

W ithout a doubt, my favorite movie of all time is,
"Support Your Local Sheriff" starring James Garner,
Joan Hackett, Jack Elam, and Henry Morgan. In this movie,
James Garner is just passing through a lawless town and is
asked by the town's people to be their sheriff. Garner insists
that he was "Just passing through on his way to Australia"
and could not possibly stay. He added that he had read
about it in a book and decided that he wanted to go there.

I found myself saying to myself and others, "I am just
passing through on my way to new Jerusalem." I have not

seen it on a map, but read about it in the Bible and I definitely want to go there and take others there with me. Like a Holy Land tour, if you get enough people to go with you, your trip is free. In this case, Jesus has already paid for the trip and everyone has the chance to go. The cross was the price our Lord paid for our journey to someday be with him in heaven.

Life has been described as a "journey" and we all are on this trip and hopefully and yes, prayerfully, we all end up at heaven's gate. It's not advertised as a resort but described very clearly as paradise in the Gospel of John, and again in Revelation. I am reminded that, we start our journey at the foot of the cross of Jesus Christ and all travel plans are placed in his hands.

Some years ago, Onda and I took a trip to California to visit our daughter, Tami, and her family. We would first drive to Colorado Springs, Colorado to visit our son, Everett, and his family, then take a bus from Denver on to Los Angeles. This way, we could enjoy the scenery and leave the driving to someone else. Rather than take a plane, this trip would allow us to see the mountains and desert.

The short bus trip to Denver was uneventful and pretty quick but when we got to the Denver bus terminal, we thought we were in a circus. We were greeted by a man who could have been a ring master. He was directing passengers like a traffic cop and after taking one look at us and sizing us up, says, "Welcome to Sociology 101." He asked us where we were headed and we said, "California, to see our kids." He then asked, "Why by bus?" I replied, "So we can see the country." He then led us to the right bus that was being loaded and laughingly said, "Enjoy!"

By this time, we were asking each other, "Lord, did we make a mistake?" The thought was, we cancel this plan and get a taxi to take us to the airport. Somehow, the bus driver interceded and managed to get us a seat directly behind him after moving some people around. He said, "This way I can keep an eye on you!"

To this day, we are completely sure why he felt that way and we enjoyed talking with him during the trip. Onda ended up supplying him with wet wipes and paper napkins that she had in her purse. Being in the front of the bus, we did not at first see the folks making the journey with us. Many had bed rolls, pillows, cardboard boxes secured with rope, and an assortment of food and drinks. If one is familiar with pictures of bus travel in Africa, this is how it felt. Fortunately, there was no one sitting on top of the bus and there was, I think, no chickens or goats.

We had little contact with our fellow travelers, except for the bus driver and a black gentleman who sat across the aisle from us. He introduced himself as "Ben" and that he was returning to Las Vegas after visiting relatives in New York. For the next several hours, Ben shared that he was a retired army Sargent and had moved to Las Vegas because he liked the excitement of living in a "city that never sleeps." When we told him that we had just visited our son, who was an army captain, we did not run out of things to talk about.

We thought we had said our "goodbyes" when we arrived at the Las Vegas bus terminal. We had about an hour layover and we were surprised that Ben returned to ask us if he could show us around. We replied that we didn't want to venture far from the bus station and Ben said that would not be necessary. We followed him just a few steps and found ourselves in a gambling casino, complete with a bar, dining tables, and gambling machines. Ben insisted that we join him at the bar and offered to buy us a drink. I thought to myself, "We're just passing through on the way to New Jerusalem," so I told Ben, "Onda and I would enjoy a Coke." There on the bar was a mechanical poker game machine and Ben pulled out a pocket of change and told Onda that she could play poker and he would help her.

Onda very graciously excused herself by saying that she would rather watch him. Ben was enjoying his drink and apparently, was surprised that he continued to win game after game. He told Onda that she really brought him good luck. Finally, he excused himself, but returned in minutes with shrimp cocktails and told us that they were really good here. We had never eaten shrimp at 3:00 a.m. before, but they were good, and we thanked him for being so generous and gracious.

It was at this point that we explained that our bus would be leaving shortly, and I reached into my pocket and handed him a little cross. I said, "Ben, God loves you and we do too. You've been great and we would not have experienced this part of Las Vegas had it not been for you." Ben looked at the cross for some time. Bowing and shaking his head, he looked up with a tear in his eye and asked, "What do you do?" I replied that I used to be a cop, but for the past several years, I was a United Methodist minister. Ben continued to look at the cross, which says, "God Loves You!" and said, "This is what I needed...what I have been looking for."

Ben walked us to our bus and hugged us both and asked us to please write him and let him know that we made it to our daughter's okay. By now, we had some "sweaty eyeballs," and we exchanged addresses and assured him that we would write.

We not only wrote Ben when we got to California, but for the next few years sent notes and cards at Christmas and Easter. Some of the most beautiful cards and notes that we have ever received were from Ben. While he never went into detail, he always thanked us for being his friends. He shared a few comments that he was going to a Methodist church and the fact that his life was different now. We had always hoped that Ben would explain further in his notes what these changes were, but after sending him an Easter card and letter one year, the letter was returned to use with the word, "Deceased."

Onda and I shed some tears over Ben's death. And while the bus trip was exhausting and very different, we have long felt that we were supposed to make that particular trip, "While on the way to New Jerusalem." The Lord, we believed, had deployed us on a mission, which he would reveal only while we were on the road. This was a mission that revolved around one man, who did not ask, or did he seek, but was found by the God that truly loved him.

The journey of a Christian is defined, not only by the destination, but also by those we meet on the way. This journey really begins at the foot of the Savior's cross. The road map is the Word of God, and all our directions and instructions come from the Holy Spirit as we make our way to "New Jerusalem."

The following old church hymn sums it up pretty well.

"I'll Go Where You Want Me To Go"

IT MAY NOT BE ON THE MOUNTAIN HEIGHT
OR OVER THE STORMY SEA
IT MAY NOT BE AT THE BATTLE'S FRONT MY
LORD WILL HAVE NEED OF ME.
BUT IF, BY A STILL, SMALL VOICE HE CALLS TO
PATHS THAT I DO NOT KNOW
I'LL ANSWER, DEAR LORD, WITH MY HAND IN
THINE, I'LL GO WHERE
YOU WANT ME TO GO.
AMEN!
Mary Brown, Charles E. Prior, Carrie E. Rounsefell

Chapter Fifteen

"A SPECIAL EASTER MEMORY"

"And if the Spirit of Him who raised
Jesus from the dead is living in you, He who raised
Christ from the dead will also give life to your mortal
body through His Spirit, that lives in you."
Rom. 8:11 NIV

It was about 2:00 a.m. On an Easter morning, several years ago, the phone rang. The voice on the other end was a nurse at Decatur's St Mary's Hospital. She said she was calling on behalf of a patient's daughter, who asked her to call me and tell me that her father, Herb, was near death and would I please come to the hospital. I asked the nurse what Herb's vitals were. She replied that Herb's heart was very irregular and his blood pressure was about 60 over 30 and falling. As an EMT on an all-volunteer ambulance service, it was apparent that Herb was in cardiac shock and that I must hurry.

Before I headed for the hospital, I called my pastor friend, John Neace, to let him know that I was headed to the hospital and that I doubted I could get back in time to participate in the community Easter Sunrise service with four other churches. Since I was not scheduled to preach that morning, my part would be easily covered. I also told John how serious the man at the hospital was and asked for him and the Easter gathering to pray for him.

In Herb's hospital room, his daughter, in tears, thanked me for coming. Herb was unconscious and struggling for breath. All that could be done for him had been done and now to make him as comfortable as possible and for us, a "watch and pray time" began. It was made clear, that there was a "no code" on Herb and his daughter and I now stood at his bedside to hold his hand and pray. We talked about Herb's life and how much he was loved. As the morning wore on, Herb's daughter regained her composure and spoke gently on how her father has influenced her life. We thanked God for life, the life he gives us through the Lord Jesus and the fact that we were gathered in this little corner of the world, awaiting the first rays of the rising sun to shine through the hospital room to announce the resurrection the our Lord and Savior.

In a few moments, the announcement came as a soft light began filtering into the room. With a profound feeling of gratitude, I said to all in the room, calling out Herb's name, "Jesus is risen, and He is alive!" To our wondrous surprise, Herb opened his eyes and in a weak voice said, "And so am I!" Turning to Herb's heart monitor, it was proclaiming a dramatic change in his vitals. We all just stood there and thanked Jesus, "The Resurrection and the Life!"

Neither Herb or his daughter were members of our church, but over the next few weeks of that hospital sunrise service had changed their lives in so many ways. Before Herb left the hospital, I gave him and his daughter the small pocket cross that says, "God Loves You!" I might have missed our community Easter service and the community breakfast, but that Easter morning was so special and will always be remembered. I was reminded then and even now in Romans, "And if the Spirit of Him who raised Jesus from the dead is living in you...He will also give life to your mortal bodies through His Spirit, who lives in you!"(8:11NIV)

Herb, like Lazarus, was not resurrected, but resuscitated for His purpose. Jesus intervened in several cases like this. The marvelous fact is Jesus still works miracles and we who occasionally witness these events are forever amazed and eternally grateful. When Herb eventually died later on, there was a praise filled celebration of his life. It is felt that he had affected many lives when he shared his experience with others.

While I can't remember the exact words that were lifted in prayer, I do remember that so many times in situations like this, I always prayed that Jesus would reveal himself to what appeared to be an unconscious mind. I believe that He does show up, and through His grace, lets us know He did. Everyone one needs to know our Savior and we all need to revisit through His word, His life, Mount Calvary and spend some time at the empty tomb. The risen Christ can and will heal. Christians need to share this with others.

I am often reminded of a favorite Easter hymn,

Jesus Lives And So Shall I

JESUS LIVES AND SO SHALL I. DEATH, THY
STING GONE FOREVER: HE, WHO DEIGNED
FOR ME TO DIE, LIVES, THE BANDS OF DEATH
TO SEVER. HE SHALL RAISE ME WITH THE
JUST; JESUS IS MY HOPE AND TRUST. HE SHALL
RAISE ME WITH THE JUST.

AMEN.
Christian F. Gellert

Chapter Sixteen

"CHRISTIANS UNDER CONSTRUCTION"

"Do you want more and more of God's kindness and peace? Then learn to know Him better ... To obtain His gifts you need more than faith, you must get to know God even better to discover what He wants you to do."
2 Peter 1:2, 5 TLB

My great-grandson, Andrew, was about five years old when his mother took him to the Indianapolis Children's Museum to see a display and program about Egypt in the time of the pharaohs. He was excited about going and when he got home, he had to call his great-grandmother to tell her all about his trip. Grandma asked, "Well, what did you see?" He was even more excited when he said, "I saw three mommies all wrapped up in toilet paper and wet wipes!"

Andrew saw the Egyptian display through his world view. He described something that he had seen through his eyes and was convinced that he knew what he saw and could describe it only from his experiences in life up to this time.

It is basically true that most people perceive or understand things largely based on their experiences. As we mature in life, we tend to broaden our world view and understand life in a much larger sense. Christians are those who have met the Lord Jesus and in their own way will hopefully grow and mature in faith by making Him the Lord of their life. The scriptures tell us that our becoming a strong Christian is through a process of faith, personal growth, and guidance by the Holy Spirit. When we surrender to Christ and make Him Savior, we are to go on to make Him Lord and become a disciple of the great Carpenter who equips us with gifts and power to share our love with others. That is why Paul, in 2nd Corinthians 13:5, 7-9 writes, "Checkup on yourself. Are you really Christians? ...do you feel Christ's presence and power more and more within you? ...I pray that you will live good lives. Our greatest wish and prayer is that you will become mature Christians. And may the God of love and peace be with you." (TLB)

We are Christians under construction by the Great Builder and Author of our faith. For several years, I had a small sign on my desk which said, "Please be patient with me, God is not through with me yet." Christians are not to claim they are better than anyone else as a Pharisee did in Luke's Gospel, 18:11. The proud Pharisee prayed; "Thank God, I am not a sinner like everyone else...." Jesus made it clear to His listeners that "the proud shall be humbled, but the humble shall be honored.

At one particular Sunday morning service, I had been sharing about growth and maturing in our faith in Christ and how our actions speak volumes of our progress in our faith. I was sharing examples of our reactions when we are confronted with life's obstacles such as anger, overreacting to a situation, and also dealing with the pain of a horrific event. As always, it was "Prayer is the first response and not the last resort!" A simple, "Lord! Help!" will often suffice.

In putting this in terms of measuring maturity, the question presented to the congregation was, "How long does it take us to recover or regain composure when trouble or bad things happen to us out of the blue?" To illustrate this, I walked to the front of the congregation and noticing John sitting with his wife right on the aisle, I asked him if he could help me by standing up in front of me in the aisle. John appeared a little hesitant but when I asked him to trust me for it wasn't meant to be embarrassing, he agreed to help. As I talked about the timeline of recovering to any number of confrontations in life, we began to walk slowly toward each other. Completely unrehearsed, John and I eventuality fell into each other's arms. I will never forget that embrace, for after the service, I thanked john for helping me present the timeline aspect of recovery in a difficult situation. It was then that John shared with me that he and his wife were headed to Indiana University Hospital to undergo a heart test. I recognized this as a heart cath, to check his heart for possible blockages. I told John that I would be with him and his family the very next morning. After having prayer with him as others joined in, Onda and I changed our schedule and prepared for a three-hour drive to Indianapolis.

When we arrived at the hospital the next day, we were informed that John had started experiencing severe pain and was rushed into the lab ahead of schedule. The nurses explained that John had died and they were not able to resuscitate him. The broken-hearted family had just left to return home. I kept remembering that about 24 hours earlier, I had embraced John and now he was with Jesus. I also remembered my message about recovery in difficult situations. I confessed to the Lord that it was going to take some time to get over this day and such bad news. Now it is time to minister to the family. Prepare for a celebration of John's life. And share with what would be a grieving congregation.

The following Sunday, I had to share that even mature Christians, who trusted Christ and put all their faith in him, would eventually find peace and love, and also comfort from "The God of all Comfort." Life experience often comes with surprise and difficult challenges, but Grace comes by the Love of God in accord with His marvelous promises.

We cannot always put our lives under the microscope for understanding, but we can trust that the Lord, who loves us so much that he gave up His only Son to save us. He even saves from ourselves and continues His work in us through the power of the Holy Spirit.

Our opportunity to share God's love with others, as noted on the Little Cross in My Pocket, is a great privilege and mission given to all Christians who are to be His disciple.

"We are not ashamed of the Gospel" and as we get to know Him better and better, we also get to know ourselves. We are all Christians under construction. This is in part what the Apostle Paul meant when he said, "Work out your own salvation with fear and trembling, for it is God who works in you to will and to act according to His good purpose." (Phil. 2:12-13 NIV)

This is why the writer of 2 Peter admonishes us to work on our faith so we get to know Him better and seek the power (ability) to obtain everything, "you need for living a truly good life." We proclaim that prayer, time in His word, study, and devotion are also building foundations, which allows the Carpenter to construct us in His image and for His purposes.

2nd Peter (1:2-8) tells us we have "to work hard to discover what God wants you to do." He presents the following as a process and in growing and becoming mature in the Faith. The purpose is for us "to work hard to discover what God wants you to do." Then...

- "Learn to put aside your own desires" This is what Paul meant about dying to self.

- "This is so you will become patient and godly." We know that God is patient with us and when we share with others, "our actions will speak volumes." We will be kind and hopefully gentle as was Christ.

- "Let Christ have His way with you." The Holy Spirit was sent to equip us with every work and even give us the words to say when the need arises.

- "This will make it possible for you to enjoy people and like them, and finally you will grow to love them deeply." Jesus said, "I command you to love others even as I have loved you."(John15:12NIV)

- "The more you go on in this way, the more you will grow spiritually and become fruitful for our Lord Jesus Christ."

We are all Christians under construction and will always be. "We now have the Holy Spirit who shares His own glory... goodness might and power, which He has given to us...(complete) with all the other rich and wonderful blessings He promised!" 2 Peter 2:4

This brings me to my personal experience and understanding of not only salvation, but a desire to be "a good and faithful servant of the Lord Jesus Christ." This is why I encourage others to "pick up the cross" and follow Him as a devoted disciple.

AN AFFIRMATION OF FAITH

For me, I have personally met and fallen in love with the Lord Jesus Christ and have made Him the Lord of my life. It is He whom I serve, and I desire to be all the things He wants me to be. I admit that I have yet to arrive, but gladly accept the fact that, I like others, am a Christian under construction and in the hands of the Carpenter Himself. It is for that reason; I choose to be the Carpenter's helper and all I have shared or will share is about Him and Him alone. I carry the "Little Cross in My Pocket" to remind me of that fact.

Chapter Seventeen

"THE LITTLE CROSS
IN YOUR POCKET"

"You are to win the hearts of faithful men (and women),
who in turn will win and train others...and as a good
soldier of Christ Jesus will follow His instructions and
satisfy the one who has enlisted you in His army."
2 Tim. 2-4 (TLB)

A famous baseball player, coach, and a homespun phi-
losopher, Yogi Berra, once proclaimed this advice,
"When you come to a fork in the road, take it!" Most people
just laugh and say they don't exactly understand what Yogi
meant, but it sure sounded funny and typical of the quips
the old baseball catcher made during his lifetime.

I am not so sure this timeless quote is always miss-un-
derstood. For me, this means when you come to a fork in
the road you have a decision to make. That is, you have to

make up your own mind which way you should go and commit to that decision and follow that path. There are probably many people who might not agree to that interpretation but to me it makes perfect sense.

Sometime, all of us will likely come to a difficult fork in the road and may have to make some really difficult decisions and then travel that path, which can be outright risky or considered dangerous. It is really a difficult decision when you are not sure where you are, how you should stand, or where you are headed.

Years ago, before my father went to be with the Lord, he and I were sharing war stories. He, for a long time, was hesitant as a World War II Navy veteran to share what were horrific stories but as he got older, he opened up and shared some of his experiences. I think he enjoyed hearing my stories of being a police officer and agent involved in criminal investigations.

After listening to some of the details of his being in the Pacific during those war time years, I asked my father, "It must have been hard not knowing where you were most of the time and not knowing where you were going?" He quickly replied, "Oh, we all knew where we were! We were right behind Admiral Halsey, fleet commander, trying to keep up." "But how did you know where you were going?" Dad said, "We did! We were headed to the next battle with the enemy. We were trying to find them and them us."

My father had ended up on Okinawa and was involved in a deadly battle fighting off enemy suicide planes. When I asked him about watching these planes trying to sink his ship, he replied, "I never saw much. I was so busy feeding 20mm shells into the gun to look around." He added that he loaded the gun faster than the gunner could shoot. Fortunately, the war ended before the entire fleet would have headed for the island of Japan. He admitted, with tears in his eyes, that he and his shipmates were "scared to death". Had the war not ended when it did, our country's path to victory would have ended with hundreds of thousands of American and Japanese deaths. When I remarked to my father about how all of those battles had to have pushed so many to the very limit of their ability to fend off the constant threat of severe injury or death, he replied that, "It was our duty. And even as bad as it was, I would do it all over again to protect my family and country."

Jesus told his disciples, to "Go and make disciples of all nations...teach them to obey everything I have commanded you." And then the promise, "And surely I am with you always, to the very end of the age". Matt. 28:18-20 NIV He told them to, "Pick up your cross and follow me." Luke 14:27 NIV And still, He would be with them...and with us.

While some have read this "cross" as a particular trial, a sickness perhaps, personal conflict, it is clear that the cross Jesus was actually talking about was the cross of burden that we would carry for others. It was because we are to love others even as Christ had loved us. The cross of Christ was carried for the life of the world. The cross we carry is likewise, for the life of the world.

Our cross was our fork in the road as we became Christians and devoted disciples. Jesus didn't say, "Well friends! I want you to consider telling others about me." He said, "Get on with the mission! The Great Commission in Matthew 28 is the mission." And we were not sent without weaponry or preparation. We have the cross, the blood of Christ, the spiritual gifts of the Holy Spirit, the Word of God, our testimony, and authority to complete our mission. It was for us "to win the hearts of the faithful and train them up to do likewise." As Paul told Timothy, "Be a good soldier and be ready to suffer because of our duty to obey." He never said it would be easy, but that we would have joy eventually by carrying our cross.

While I have shared several experiences. I have only shared the following a few times over the years. I once had a terror-filled nightmare some years ago in which I dreamed that I was walking along a mucky river and noticed that there was a man walking on the other side. This man was on the bank but there was a horrible looking beast in the water right beside the man as he walked. The man kept petting this creature with his hand and kept walking and talking to it. The man had come to the end of the river and left the beast in the water but as he continued walking, the monster jumped up out of the water and pulled him back into the water.

Needless to say I awoke from this very vivid nightmare sweating and feeling very afraid. I quickly responded with a prayer asking the Lord to show me the meaning of the dream that I had just experienced. Just as quickly the Lord answered me "None of my followers can ever make friends with the devil and remain a faithful disciple." You can't love the Lord and the world at the same time. Soldiers can't get entangled in civilian pursuits, athletes can't forego training or the contest and farmers can get no yield without the hard work of sowing and reaping. Christians can't go on with dual-citizenship forever.

Our citizenship is in the Kingdom of God and this is the address on the passport of our soul. Our love and devotion to duty is the summation of all the good that we can do which can force open the jaws of the beast and release us from its grip.

It is the love and grace of God that leads us to victory and joy. With this understanding of the dream I returned to sleep in perfect peace. I always remember that Satan is and always will be our deadly enemy.

"This is the Little Cross in your Pocket": the cross in one's heart that we carry a special burden and love for others. One final thought to be passed on to the family of God, that is, of the vital importance of sharing Christ with our own family members. It is so heartbreaking to have a family member come and ask when their loved one dies, "Do you know if he or she went to heaven when they died?" Again, this is so sad when those who remain do not know whether this special person in their lives went to be with the Lord or the other place. All I have been able to share so often is that I know for sure God loved their loved one and us as well. I know God will come to comfort us in our doubts and with our difficult questions. God is a forgiving God and I believe a lot of people have a faith which may have included a personal relationship with the Lord. What is sad is not sharing with our loved ones of that faith. Then too, we should have a burden to share our faith with our loved ones who may find it difficult to speak of their personal, private life and share such intimacy.

Going back to the things my grandfather taught me about speaking to the heart, I also learned to listen to the hearts of all, and especially new Christians. And share the victory we have over the threats we face as being disciples, servants and better yet, true soldiers

I have never forgotten those years ago, some in our United Methodist Church strongly suggested that as we prepared new hymnals for our congregations, we should remove those hymns that included anything that mentioned war, battles, soldiers, fortresses, etc. We have to remember we have an enemy and there will be battles to fight. Thankfully, many if not most of these hymns remain in the church hymnal. To even think we would omit these words was worrying:

"Onward Christian soldiers, marching as to war,
With the cross of Jesus, going on before."
Sabine Baring–Gould

Just as the birth, the life, the death of Christ on the cross, and the Resurrection and victory of the Lord Jesus Christ was never meant to be some kind of well-kept secret, God's plan to save the entire world has been given to us both by word and testimony. Even if we are confronted by evil and the evil one, we are equipped to fend off such attacks by the evil rulers of the unseen world. "We will sing sacred songs, making music in our hearts to the Lord, being filled with the Holy Spirit and always giving thanks for everything to our God and Father in the name of our Lord Jesus Christ." (Eph5:19-20NIV)

For over five decades, Onda and I have seen the miracles of salvation and the growth progress of so many. The "Little Cross in my Pocket" has been presented to many and what a joy to have those Christians come back and say, "I had to give my cross away to someone who needed it so badly. Can I have another?" We have seen congregations come alive with the love of Christ, who witnessed to others and not just invite them to church. The prayer meetings, studies, and even role playing which presented a biblical approach while sharing our intimate relationship to Christ, the young people who grew in their relationship to even take their Bibles to school, witness to others, and through their witness bring friends to church and youth gatherings. Even some youth who attended early morning worship at another church across the street from one of our churches would run after their worship service to join their friends in our worship service and perform in some of the plays they all would write to present to the whole congregation. They wanted to share their faith.

This is our joy and it is our strength. For those who said that they did not have the courage to speak or pray in front of others, to respond to prayer by giving testimony and praying out loud in front of others. To see the victory come for those who had spiritual battles with powers of darkness who whispered in their ears that they were not even Christians and that God didn't love them. To be told that they were crazy and that nobody would believe them. The evil one was made powerless!

This again is what it means to win the hearts of others and train them up in the faith. This begins with our own love ones, especially our children. We are to tell them that we love and care for them and that we will be there for them. This may well save them and others from the jaws of the beast. The evil one is held powerless. This is the cross we carry.

JESUS SETTLED THIS AT THE CROSS!

"What Is In Your Pocket?"

Jesus has made it clear that when we pick up our cross and follow Him that it would be risky for there would be dangers, trials and possibly suffering. He told all His disciples; "I am sending you out like lambs among wolves." (Luke 10:3) NIV. "You will be my witnesses...even to the ends of the earth." (Acts 1:8NIV) When we give the Master Charge of our life, that cross we carry can be found in the pocket of our heart. It is a gift of love which includes a concern, a burden for others that declares "God Loves You"....He loves all of us and we can say to others to whom we share;
"Yes! I Love You Too!"

May our Loving God give us all, this special gift that we let the whole world know that Jesus is Lord, to the glory of our heavenly Father.

Grace to all and peace from God our Father!

THE LITTLE CROSS
IN MY POCKET

Acknowledgements

Contributing Editor: Matthew Lyon

Editors: Rachel Lyon and Tami Koch

Poem: "The Cross In My Pocket" by Verna Thomas, Agora, Inc. ©All Rights Reserved Used By Permission.

Crosses: Persons interested in purchasing the crosses shown onthe cover and mentioned throughout the book can visit or contact Agora; a Christian owned and operated business for fifty years at **www.crossinmypocket.com** or at P.O. Box 724 Fairburn, GA 30213, Phone (800) 354-9406.

Use of Names: Many names have been changed to protect the privacy of individuals. Juveniles, in the Juvenile Court system, are legally protected by law and names were all changed to protect their identity.

Scripture Texts:

Scripture quotations marked (TLB) are taken from the "Living Bible. Copyright c 1971. Used by permission of Tyndale House Publishers, a division of Tyndale House Ministries, Carol Stream, Illinois. 60188, All rights reserved

Scripture quotations marked (NIV) are taken from The Holy Bible, New International Version r NIV r Copyright c 1973, 1978, 1984 by International Bible Society r Used by permission. All rights reserved worldwide.

Scripture quotations marked (RSV) are taken from the Revised Standard Version of the Bible, copyright 1952 (2nd edition, 1971) by the Division of Christian Education

of the National Council of the Churches of Christ in the United States of America.

Used by permission. All rights reserved.

Use of Hymns:

Most church hymns are found in enumerable hymnals throughout the world. The following church hymns are in the public domain and can be found in The United Methodist Hymnal, 1996, Methodist Publishing house,

"Trust and Obey" by James H. Sammis, 1887, listed on page 378.

"Amazing Grace" by John Newton, 1779, listed on page 378.

"In The Garden" by C. Austin Miles, 1912. listed on page 314.

"Onward Christian Soldiers" by Sabina Baring-Gold, listed on page 575.

CPSIA information can be obtained
at www.ICGtesting.com
Printed in the USA
BVHW081125070321
601861BV00007B/126

9 781632 215383